After You've Said I Do

A Guide to the Early Years of Marriage.

Hardy R. Denham, Jr.

Revised Edition

ISBN: O-939298-18-X

PRINTED IN UNITED STATES OF AMERICA

CONTENTS

FOREWORD . . . . .Page 7

Chapter 1—HOW DO I LOVE THEE? . . . . .Page 9
       —What Is This Thing Called Love?
       —A Profile of Marital Love
       —How to Nurture Your Love

Chapter 2—LISTEN TO MY MOUTH . . . . .Page 23
       —Sending and Receiving
       —Difficulties in Communicating
       —Five Essential Factors

Chapter 3—DON'T TREAD ON ME! . . . . .Page 41
       —The Crisis of Conflict
       —The Control of Conflict
       —The Conduct for Conflict

Chapter 4—THE BEDROOM BLESSING . . . . .Page 57
       —God Said, "It's Good"
       —Is Sex That Important?
       —Ways to Make It Great

Chapter 5—TO BUY OR NOT TO BUY? . . . . .Page 75
       —Financial Follies
       —Marital Money Management
       —Priceless Principles

FOREWORD

I've been the father of the bride—twice. Of course, my major contribution as the father of the bride was to sign the checks. However, I did get a "father's-eye-view" of the plans and preparations that go into a wedding ceremony. As a minister and pastor, I knew something about this, but when the bride is your daughter you really get to see the inside workings of a formal wedding.

Weeks, and sometimes months, go into the planning and preparation for a formal wedding. All that time is spent for a ceremony that consumes about twenty minutes at the most and a reception that probably consumes a little more than twice that amount of time. But after the vows are exchanged amidst the flicker of candles and organ music, then what? What do you do after you've said, "I do?"

My concern as one involved in scores of weddings is not so much that all goes as planned during the brief ceremony, but what happens afterward. A beautiful wedding ceremony makes for a lovely memory, but that memory becomes a nightmare if the marriage sours.

An acquaintance told me she had gotten married. I responded, "I didn't know that. I guess I wasn't invited to the wedding." She replied, "You could have come in my place."

In May, 1981, the *Boston Free Press* reported the results of a survey on marriage. Seventy percent of all couples interviewed said they would not marry the same mates if they had the opportunity to marry again.[1] The staggering divorce rate in this country, coupled with the indications of so much matrimonial misery, presents a sad picture of the state of marriage today.

These facts have led some people to conclude that marriage as a life relationship should be junked in favor of newer, more flexible and less binding life styles. The problem, however, is not with the institution, but with the individuals involved. To put it bluntly, marriage is what you make it.

In the following chapters I've endeavored to deal with matters that are vital in making a happy marriage. Notice the words— making a happy marriage. This means that such a marriage doesn't just happen but is made to happen. Whether you will have one or not is dependent on a number of factors about you, your mate, how compatible you are, the expectations you bring to marriage, and the like. However, I firmly believe that what kind of marriage you have is also determined by what the two of you do after you've said, "I do."

I have several purposes in mind in writing this book. First, since the wedding ceremony formally and officially begins the adventure of making a marriage, this book is for couples who are planning to launch out in that venture. Much of the material in the book is taken from, and is an elaboration of, a pre-marital counseling syllabus I use in talking with couples who are planning to marry.

Second, this is also a book for those who have already said, "I do." This isn't intended to be a marriage manual, but I believe it can be used by a couple to help and guide in their determination to make a marriage happy.

Third, the book is offered as a help to pastors for use in pre-marital counseling. The material can be adapted to a minister's own counseling approach, or the book itself can be used as a study guide in dealing with couples.

With these purposes in mind, I offer the material in this book. As already indicated, it is by no means the final or most definitive word on the subjects about which I've written. However, what I've written is factually based and reflects the wisdom and understanding gained through study and by being exposed professionally to both the best and the worst in marriages.

Endnotes:

1. *Moody Monthly* (June 1982; Volume 82, Number 9), p. 17.

1
How Do I Love Thee?

"I'll be loving you always,
With a love that's true, always."

These are lines from a beautiful love song that was often sung at weddings. In your own distinctive way you've probably said to each other, "I'll always love you." But a beautiful wedding with the music of love, and the verbal affirmations of love, doesn't guarantee that the two of you will always be "in love." After all, the couples involved in the more than one million divorces annually in America probably said "I love you" to each other—and in most cases, they probably meant it at the time. The tragic termination of their marital relationship is a declaration that something happened to their love. It declares that love can die. Every time a judge's gavel falls with the two words, "Divorce granted," it is an announcement that two people's love story has come to an end.

Why does this happen? Dr. Ed Wheat, M.D., answered, "Surely it is because the 'lovers' have no clear understanding of what love is and is not; they do not know how to love; and in many cases they have never made the commitment to love."[1]

Hopefully, it was love that led you to the marriage altar, but keeping love alive and healthy in your marriage is up to you. That's what this chapter is all about. It deals with love and how to make it a growing experience in your relationship.

What Is This Thing Called Love?

We talk about love, write songs about it, and compose poems about it—but what is it? Is love some indefinable feeling that sweeps over you like a wave when, during some enchanted evening, you meet the person that's right for you? In answering the question, "How do I love thee?", we must first define what we're talking about.

Any attempt to define love is complicated by the fact that the word is used in such a variety of ways. A man may say to his wife, "I love you," and also declare, "I love football." Certainly he doesn't mean the same thing, even though some wives wonder which he loves most during the football season. A woman may say, "I love my children," and also say, "I love to cook." Again the same word is used but with an obviously different meaning.

One dictionary lists as many as twenty-five different definitions of the word love. The word is used to describe everything from the highest sacrifice to the most shameful form of lust. Kay K. Arvin wrote about the word:

> "This poor beat-up, bruised, and beautiful little word is hooked on to a lot of emotions to which it isn't even a distant cousin. It is handy because it can add a certain amount of dignity to undignified skullduggery—like personal gratification, the need of one person to possess another, physical desire, even convenience."[2]

The fact is that our concepts of love have been influenced more by the entertainment media than by experience. Many people have a make-believe concept of love that falls apart when put to the test and tension of day-to-day living.

In answering the question, "What is love?", one must recognize that love is not biological but psychological. The proof of this is in the fact that even though every person in the world has the same basic chemical composition and biological structure as you; they don't all feel about the special one in your life the way you do. What makes the difference? It isn't something in the body, but in the mind. It isn't biological but psychological.

Love is an intense positive interest in another person. This means that love is not easy and simple, or simply a matter of "doing what comes naturally." Instead, it is an active force controlled by the

10

Many people have a
make-believe concept of
love that falls apart
when put to the test and
tension of day-to-day
living.

will. Pat Clendinning wrote: "Real love, mature love, comes about when I discover someone whose needs I want to meet, and whom I want to help meet my own needs."[3] Love is a choice backed up by action that involves a cost. It is the recognition of special value in another, the choice to affirm that value, and the acts consistent with the best interest of the person loved. Love involves feelings which range all the way from "thrills to sweet tranquility."[4] Thus, love relates to a person's mind and will, as well as emotions.

This means that love is not something we fall into and fall out of. This lack of understanding about love is reflected in the statement of a much-married Hollywood actress. She said, "You fall in love—you fall out of love. When you fall out of love it is better to change partners and remain friends than to stay together and grow to hate each other."[5]

Actually we grow into love, yet love has the potential to die. Stop and think about how you came to be "in love" with the significant other in your life. Either in your first meeting, or through association, you saw qualities in the person that appealed to you. You responded in a positive manner to the person, and that led to further discoveries of qualities and characteristics you liked. As your positive attitude toward the person grew, love was born. It wasn't something you fell into, but an experience you grew into.

There are three types of love in marriage. These are the sensual, the companionship and the giving love. These three types of love are usually identified with three Greek words: *eros, philia,* and *agape.*

The first type, the sensual, is sexual love. It is inspired by the biological structure of human nature. It has its foundation in the physical urge which seeks fulfillment in sexual union. A good marriage doesn't exist long without it. The husband and wife in a good marriage will love each other erotically and sensuously. This involves more than just sexual intercourse. It includes all the loving expressions of our maleness and femaleness. H. Norman Wright described *eros* love as: "The lingering touch of the fingers; the deep kiss; candles and music at dinner; the 'I promise you' wink; a low whistle when she models a new dress; giving her a sheer negligee for her birthday; wearing it for him that night."[6]

The second type of love, companionship, is expressed in the delight and joy experienced in each other's company. We were cre-

12

ated with a need for companionship. In the beginning God saw that it wasn't good for man to be alone.[7] Companionship love includes the sharing of common goals and interests. It means that the husband and wife "like" each other as well as love each other. They express this love by doing things together as well as just being together. "While eros is almost a face-to-face relationship, philia is very often a shoulder-to-shoulder relationship."[8]

The third and highest form of love is giving love. *Agape* love is gift-love. It is not just something that happens to you, but something you make happen. It is not a love that reacts, but acts. It isn't a whim of the emotions, but an act of the will. It's the giving of yourself to another, not because the person to whom you give yourself is deserving or responds to you in a positive way, but because you choose to give. This is the love that goes on loving even when the one loved is not acting lovable. It isn't feeling love, but doing love. Rick Yohn described how the ancient Greeks used this word *agape*: "(*Agape*) included the emotions but wasn't limited by them. It included a natural affection, but even when it wasn't natural to love, *agape* loved anyway. This love provided an excellent basis for companionship, but it transcended that phase if the companion failed to love in return."[9]

Agape love is the love patterned after Christ's love for us.[10] This kind of gift-love, or giving love, is the only love that can hold a marriage together over the years. When a couple ceases freely to give to each other, companionship sours and sensual love becomes an exercise in exploitation.

A Profile of Marital Love

Having given a definition of love, let's now consider how this love is to be expressed in your relationship as husband and wife. There are seven factors in this profile of marital love. The order in which they are presented is not to be taken as a ranking in order of importance but as a way of looking at one object from seven different vantage points.

First, marital love is a responsiveness to the total self of the person loved. We are composite creatures. Our personhood is expressed spiritually, physically, mentally and emotionally. Marital love recognizes the diversity of one's being and responds positively to all facets of that being. For example, a husband is to love his wife's body, but at the same time respect and treasure the personality represented by that body.

Second, in marital love one is to think more of the happiness of one's mate than of one's self. People are not to marry to find happiness, but to give it. Tragically, many people today marry in order to find happiness. In former times, people married for more down-to-earth reasons, and if it turned out that they were happy in their marriage, it was a bonus. Now the desire for happiness is a major motive in getting married. The consequence of this is that if the one who marries seeking happiness doesn't experience it, he ends the marriage and looks for another mate who will make him happy. Happiness is not the purpose of marriage, but it surely can be the result of a good marriage. The husband's primary desire should be the happiness of his wife, and the wife's main goal should be the happiness of her husband. If this is true in your marriage, neither of you will lose. But when each is seeking to gain happiness rather than to give it, both can lose.

Third, in marital love mates accept responsibility for each other's needs. Men and women obviously bring needs to marriage. The fact that we marry is itself expressive of a need. In bringing needs to marriage we expect that these will be met. Even though some of our need-expectancy may be unrealistic, other needs are legitimate and should be met.

A need is something you have which is vital to wholeness in being. H. Norman Wright wrote: "The amount of satisfaction that you experience in your marriage is directly related to the fulfillment of your needs."[11] Abraham Maslow developed a "hierarchy of needs" in which he identified five basic needs. These are: physical needs (the things we need to sustain life); safety or security; love; self-esteem; and self-actualization. In a real sense, the first four needs must be met before the individual can meet his own need to realize the full potential of his personhood by giving himself to another.

William Glasser wrote that our most basic need is to love and to be loved. A healthy marriage, therefore, is one in which both partners recognize the need of each to be loved and valued, and then allow each to love the other in return. When mates have the degree of love that willingly accepts another's needs as a personal responsibility, and willingly gives to meet them, neither partner ends up left out.

14

Fourth, husbands and wives who love each other as they should know joy in each other's company and experience pain in separation. Mates who have a maturing love for each other enjoy being together, and feel that a part of themselves is missing when they are separated. Marriage was God's answer to man's aloneness in the beginning.[12] It results in a togetherness that not only completes one's personhood, but also provides enjoyable companionship.

Fifth, marital love involves mutual enjoyment that is expressed. In marriage a husband and wife become "one flesh."[13] This is an obvious reference to physical union. As shall be seen in Chapter 4, sex is a multi-purpose gift of God. One aspect of your physical union, however, should be the expressed delight in each other's bodies.

Sixth, marital love is positive in attitude. Instead of looking for faults in another, it magnifies virtues. Your love isn't to be blind in that it doesn't see imperfections in your mate, but it is to be kind in that it doesn't dwell on them.

Finally, in marital love there is a feeling of belonging. Marriage is a commitment of two lives to each other. In that commitment the husband and wife say to each other, "I now belong to you." That commitment becomes a feeling of belonging that makes life for you a duet, not a solo experience.

How to Nurture Your Love

I have described love as a growth process. One grows into love. Your love life didn't just happen—it was made to happen. Because you chose to do certain things, you came to love the significant other in your life. Now what? Does this mean that love, having come to be, will always remain? Absolutely not! That is, not unless you see to it that it does not perish.

I've heard husbands and wives say, "You can't always act like you're still on a honeymoon." Usually this is a reaction to a demand for more romance in the marriage. My response to that statement is, "Why not?" Of course, you have to settle down to a daily routine. Moonlight and roses must leave time for daylight and dishwater. Life together becomes daily but it doesn't have to be drab. You can keep the honeymoon spirit alive in your marriage, and thereby continue to grow in your love for each other.

I've never been much of a gardener. In fact, the most successful thing I've been able to grow in my yard is a healthy crop of weeds. But I know that plants are living things and their health and growth

15

are dependent upon daily care and attention. I've heard that the belief that plants respond to being talked to kindly is because of the carbon dioxide expelled in the breath when one talks. In other words, by talking to a plant a person gives something of himself that nurtures the plant. In a similar way, love grows and blossoms like a beautiful plant as we continue to do things that nourish it. Each couple should discover and develop unique and special ways to do this. These techniques are vast in number. In fact, I have two little books in my library with titles that suggest this. One is named *365 Ways To Say "I Love You,"* and the second is *365 More Ways To Say "I Love You."* These books indicate that there are many ways couples can nourish and grow in their love.

At this point, I am going to suggest some basic ways to do this that are not to be overlooked. I admit that these are not profound, but at the same time they are vitally important. In fact, I consider them to be imperatives in a growing and developing love life.

First, speak your love. This is common for couples to do in the courtship period of their relationship, and should be even more so after the wedding. The couple who assumes that each knows how the other feels, thus dispensing with verbal affirmations of love, is playing the fool. Love wants to be told what love already knows.

As a husband, you need to remember that it is largely what you say and how you say it that prompts either response or rejection by your wife. She responds to verbal affirmations of love and appreciation. A poet wrote:

> "A woman never tires of hearing,
> 'I love you,' said in words endearing.
> She'll hear it when she first gets up,
> And again over the breakfast cup;
> And then again by phone at noon,
> And while dancing to an off-key croon.
> Although she hears it day and night,
> She never comes to think it trite."

I would quickly add, dear wife, that what is true of you is also true of your husband. Even though his response to you is more visual than verbal, the average husband needs to know he's loved and appreciated.

Second, show little courtesies. Again it is commonplace in courtship for couples to be courteous and gracious towards each other.

There is nothing in the wedding ceremony that says this is to end with "I do." After all, it was these little things that endeared you to your mate. The continuation of them after marriage is even more necessary because they ease the tensions marriage can generate.

Third, make time for togetherness. Life makes its demands on husbands and wives, and usually in an increasing degree as they grow older. For him it is the demands of business coupled with church and civic responsibilities. For her it is home, children and social obligations. One tragedy in American marriages today is that in the course of time many couples come to face each other after the children are gone and the business is established, and they discover that they are strangers. In the process of responding to other demands they neglected each other.

A man's business is important. After all, it is by means of it that he provides for the material needs of his family. But his relationship to his wife is more important. The children can be demanding in terms of time and energy and leave a wife feeling washed out physically and mentally at the end of the day. But in a definite way the husband is more important than the children. After all, one day the children will be grown and gone and he's all she'll have.

Finding time together often calls for creative planning, but it can be done. Furthermore, the quantity of time involved is as important as the quality. It's both how much time you have together and how well you use it.

Fourth, maintain personal attractiveness. Even though we can put too much emphasis on physical appearance, in many cases it was the cause for your initial attraction to the one you love.

I have a conviction that how one dresses and looks is not only a reflection of what the person thinks of himself, but what he thinks of those who have to look at him. This applies to husbands and wives in the home as much as to the people you meet on the street or in the store and in the office.

"Father Knows Best" was a popular family show on television years ago and is still seen as reruns on some channels today. In watching the program, I am amused at how Robert Young and Jane Wyatt, the parents in the show, were dressed in home situations. Even though their attire was far more formal than was true in the average situation at the time, it's a lot better than what I've seen in some homes. Wise is the wife who takes time out for a little "repair work" before hubby comes home in the evening. And wise is the

17

husband who looks as neat, though maybe not as well dressed, on his day off as he does when he goes out to meet the public.

Finally, accentuate the positive in your mate. In courtship the average couple puts the best foot forward and does their best to conceal their less commendable characteristics, but marriage has a way of opening closed closets. In time the wife discovers that her knight has some rusty spots on his shining armor, and he discovers that she isn't quite as "perfect" as he first thought. It's very easy for mates to begin to focus on these flaws. Such excessive negativism will sour your relationship and can eventually strangle your love.

Some couples drift into a mental or emotional neutrality toward each other. They begin to take each other for granted. The mate is just someone who's around, much like some appliance in the house.

Shirley Rice wrote words to wives expressive of this positive approach you should take toward the one you love:

> "Are you in love with your husband? Not, do you love him? I know you do. He has been around a long time, and you're used to him. He is the father of your children. But are you in love with him? How long has it been since your heart really squeezed when you looked at him? Look at him through another woman's eyes—he still looks pretty good, doesn't he? Why is it you have forgotten the things that attracted you to him at first? This is an attitude we drift into—we take our men for granted. We complain bitterly about this ourselves because we hate to be taken for granted. But we do this to them."[14]

Wise is the couple who expresses gratitude and continues to look for the best in each other daily. Everyone has both strong and weak points. Magnify the strong while minimizing the weak. Remember, love is a positive response to another person, not a negative one. If you are to grow in your love life you must continually accentuate the positive and eliminate the negative.

I began this chapter with the question, "How do I love thee?" Hopefully I've conveyed the truth that how you love is up to you. There's nothing automatic about love. In the truest sense, love is something you do. How you do it determines the degree of marital happiness you will experience.

Publicist Frank Wright wrote hundreds of love poems to his wife, some of which he published in a little book, *Hi Sweetie!* He wrote: "The longer we are married the more I see that happiness in marriage doesn't just happen. Let's always hold hands and tell each other of our love. Let's never take each other for granted. Let's 'give in' with a spirit of joy. That's what we have been doing and it works, doesn't it?"[15]

It does work, and it will work for you, too.

Endnotes:

1. Ed Wheat, M.D. *Love Life.* Grand Rapids: Zondervan Publishing House, 1980, p. 47.
2. Kay K. Arvin. *1 + 1 = 1.* Nashville: Broadman Press, 1969, pp. 123–124.
3. Pat Clendinning. "What Marriage Is All About," *Home Life.* Nashville: June 1982, p. 10.
4. Wheat. op. cit., p. 46.
5. Ibid., p. 48.
6. H. Norman Wright. *The Pillars of Marriage.* Glendale, CA: Regal Books, 1980, pp. 80–81.
7. Genesis 2:18.
8. Wright. op. cit., p. 82.
9. Rick Yohn. *Beyond Spiritual Gifts.* Wheaton, IL: Tyndale Publishing House, 1976, p. 27.
10. John 13:34.
11. Wright. op cit., p. 67.
12. Genesis 2:18.
13. Genesis 2:24.
14. Shirley Rice. *Physical Unity in Marriage.* Norfolk, VA: The Tabernacle Church of Norfolk, 1973, pp. 3–4.
15. Wheat. op. cit., p. 53.

NOTES

NOTES

NOTES

2
Listen To My Mouth

A good friend of mine frequently prefaces something about to be said with the statement, "Listen to my mouth." These four words send the signal that an important message is about to be communicated. I like the phrase, "Listen to my mouth," for in its simplicity it expresses some of the complexity of communication.

The importance of communication cannot be minimized. It is an absolute "must" in relationships at all levels and in all areas of life. Communication has been described as the glue that holds a relationship together. In no relationship, however, is communication more important than in marriage. It has been said that "Marriage is one long conversation, hopefully seasoned with understanding."[1]

Communication is recognized by marriage counselors as the number one problem or cause of problems in marriage. If a couple is able to communicate with each other, they can effectively deal with any problem they face, but if they can't communicate, anything can quickly become a problem.

Lou Beardsley stressed the importance of communication in marriage when she wrote: "Communication is the lifeblood of a marriage; without it, the relationship becomes terminally ill and eventually dies." She added, "Most divorces occur because somewhere along the line, communication has broken down between marriage partners."[2]

What a shame it is that so many courtships which began with almost constant talking end in marriages of silence. It's hard to believe that the same two people who never tired of talking to each other now sit for hours in the same room with little more than grunts and growls in each other's direction. Little wonder they wake up one morning to discover that they're total strangers with no basis whatever for a fulfilling and satisfying relationship.

Because communication is so vitally important in your marital relationship it must be persistently and patiently practiced. Good communication is a skill and like any skill it must be continually used and improved or else it will deteriorate. The importance of communication in your marriage, along with some dangers and essentials in the communication process, is what this chapter addresses.

Sending and Receiving

Communication is the process of sending and receiving messages. That's a very simple definition, and having given it, I must add that the definition is about all that's simple in communication. The complexity of the communication process is indicated in the definition given by H. Norman Wright: "Communication is a process (either verbally or non-verbally) of sharing information with another person in such a way that he understands what you are saying. *Talking* and *listening* and *understanding* are all involved in the process of communication."[3]

The practice of communication includes any kind of thought, feeling or information passed between people. It's the process of sharing with another your ideas, interests, feelings and knowledge in a manner that makes it possible for the receiver to understand the message being sent.

It's frequently stated that there are three general means of communicating a message. These are verbal, non-verbal and symbolic. The first employs words as the vehicles of communication, and is the most direct means of communication with another. The non-verbal method involves what is often called "body language." It is communication by means of gestures, posture or facial expressions. Symbolic communication is the process of sending a message by something you do. Gifts are perhaps the most obvious method of symbolic communication, but they are by no means the only type. Non-verbal and symbolic communication have an important place in your marriage. A Chinese proverb states: "Married cou-

Because communication is so vitally important in your marital relationship it must be persistently and patiently practiced.

ples who love each other tell each other thousands of things without talking."[4]

Having defined the process of communication rather simply and identified the means by which it works, look now at the complexity of this process. Four facts need to be understood by you and your mate concerning this involved process.

First, the activity of communication ranges all the way from a simple, "Good morning," to the not-so-simple sharing of your innermost feelings and desires. John Drakeford identified seven different levels of communication.[5] These are: the greeting level; the chit-chat level; the ambivalent level ("some people give off two messages, the acceptable one and the real one"); the visceral level (i.e. the venting of hostility or frustration); the tacit or nonverbal level; the self-disclosure level; and the sexual level. John Powell listed five levels of communication in his book, *Why Am I Afraid To Tell You Who I Am?* These five levels are: cliché conversations; repeating facts about others; my ideas and judgments; my feelings and emotions; complete emotional and truthful communication.

Second, for understanding to take place in the communication process there must be more than just a common language. Certainly, you have communication problems if the speaker uses a language the hearer doesn't understand, but communication involves more than just the words used. It also includes values, attitudes, thought patterns and perceptions which give different shades of meaning to the words used. It is possible for you to hear what another person says but misunderstand completely the message if there are major differences between you and the speaker in terms of meanings.

Third, understanding as an essential in communication involves listening. We are often guilty of tuning people out. Communication experts say that the average person receives about sixteen hundred messages daily, but he acts only on about twelve of them.[6] The others are tuned out. "Do you have your ears on?" is a question used by Citizen Band radio operators. It means, "Do you have your unit turned on and are ready to receive a message?" "Having your ears on" is also essential if communication is to take place.

Listening and hearing are not the same things. Hearing can be a superficial response to sound, whereas listening involves a meaningful participation in what the speaker is saying. Hearing can be a

26

passive response while listening is an active response. Hearing words isn't the same as receiving the message. The art of listening involves more than just hearing and understanding the meaning of the words spoken. It means understanding the person. This demands "listening between the lines," or listening to pick up messages that are concealed in what is being said. This is the practice of listening "with the heart" and it involves listening for feelings.

Listening to your partner is one of the greatest things you can do for him or her. The indictment, "You're not paying attention," often means far more than simply stating that you're not listening to what he is saying. It may well mean, "You're tuning out my personhood, my presence. You're saying I'm not important." Little wonder Paul Tillich said that the first duty of love is to listen.[7]

Fourth, communication also requires response. Good communication is not a monologue in which one person does all the talking and the other listens. It's a dialogue—a channel through which messages are being sent and received by both participants. Martin Buber stated that in dialogue each partner "experiences the other side." Dwight Small wrote that "Dialogue takes place when one's very *being* confronts the *being* of the other, and when the *truth* of one life confronts the *truth* of the other."[8] Thus communication in your marriage must allow for the two of you to be senders as well as receivers.

Two additional words must be added about communication as an exercise in sending and receiving. The first is that this is a skill which is learned. It's not a process you bring to marriage ready-made. True, you know how to talk, but I hope that by now you understand that communication is far more than simply talking. Communication is a learned skill, and good communication is learned through trial and error. It's a skill which you must daily work to improve and never cease to use. You will never reach the place in your marital relationship when you can say, "I know all about my mate—what he thinks, feels, wants, needs." Both you and your mate will go through a lot of changes in which there will be new or different thought patterns, perceptions, attitudes, etc. Andre Maurois wrote: "When you marry you don't become linked to a single woman or to a single man; you are bound to all the women or all the men she or he will become."[9] This fact demands continued communication throughout your life together.

The second additional word about your process of sending and receiving is that the two of you will probably develop your own language for communication. This will be in the form of pet names for each other, veiled references and subtle allusions. These will be understood only by the two of you and no one else. Furthermore, you will also develop the ability to "hear meanings" in the things each of you do and say that others will miss. This private language can transform your communication process. By means of it, your sending and receiving will at times be a private and personal exercise in love.

Difficulties in Communicating

There is no such thing as a lack of communication. Instead, there is only inadequate or incorrect communication. We are constantly sending and receiving messages. The couple who sits in stony silence may well be communicating a great deal to each other. The problem in communication is that we often garble the message in its transmission and misinterpret it as we receive it.

The fact is that you must communicate. You can fail to communicate enough. You can communicate the wrong way. You can communicate the wrong message with the result that other people miss the meaning of the message, or misinterpret it altogether.

Husbands and wives are continually communicating with each other. David Knox wrote that "Something is always communicated, either through words or behavior. When a husband and wife are together, it is impossible for them not to communicate something, each to the other."[10] One authority has stated that a husband and wife may be exchanging as many as fifty pieces of information per second while they are together.[11] The problem with their communication is not the lack of it, but that it is often inadequate or incorrect.

The husband who comes in from work with hardly more than a nod as a greeting to his wife, slumps down in his chair and buries his head in his newspaper is communicating. He's saying that he's in a bad mood or had a disappointing day. The wife who greets her husband at the door with a frosty smile or tight-lipped hello and proceeds to bang pots and pans together as she prepares dinner is communicating. She's saying that she's had a bad day, or is angry about something he did or didn't do. In both cases the communication taking place is inadequate. Both are saying something is wrong, but they aren't saying what is wrong.

Tragically, many married couples drift into poor communication habits. In their courtship days they were so anxious to talk to each other and know what each felt, liked and wanted. But in marriage they settle down and take each other for granted. A deadly chain reaction is set in motion which not only results in poor communication, but which can easily deal a death blow to their relationship. This chain reaction is expressed in three words:

Assume—Anticipate—Apathy

Notice how this works. The couple begins to assume what each other thinks or wants. Of course, when two people live together a long time they get to know each other's minds and needs to a certain degree. But one person never fully knows what another is thinking and often real needs are concealed behind secondary or superficial ones. Thus you are on thin ice when you begin to assume with supposed accuracy what's going on inside another person.

Having assumed what each is thinking or what each wants, you then anticipate what he or she will say or do. This is an exercise in second guessing. Virginia Satir wrote: "So often partners seem so sure of each other's reactions that they do not hear or see reactions that do not fit their expectations."[12] This can easily leave both of you way out in left field. How many mates, after assuming and anticipating, have had to say apologetically, "I thought you wanted....I didn't know you needed...?"

The last stage in this reaction of communication confusion is apathy. By this, I simply mean that since a person thinks he knows what is going on inside another individual, and anticipates what will be said or done, he finally gets to the place where he really doesn't care what the other person thinks or feels. It's all over when this happens. A relationship can be maintained as long as two people are working at understanding. But when one, or both, reach the point of indifference, it's all over. In *The Cocktail Party*, T.S. Eliot describes a couple who are guilty of this deadly chain reaction. Edward said to Lavina, his wife, "One of the most infuriating things about you has always been your perfect assurance that you understood me better than I understood myself." Lavina responded:

"And the most infuriating thing about you has always been your placid assumption that I wasn't worth the trouble of understanding."

For good communication to take place there must be mutual understanding between the sender and receiver. This is easier said than done. There are so many factors which can easily short-circuit the communication process so that the receiver doesn't understand the message sent. There are at least five big difficulties encountered in the communication process with the result that the meaning is missed or misinterpreted. These are differences, definitions, distortions, distractions and deceitfulness.

First, there is the difficulty of *DIFFERENCES*. Men and women are not alike. Everyone knows that's true anatomically. But it's also true psychologically. Men and women don't always think alike; therefore, they don't always speak alike. Men usually think and speak objectively, while women are more emotional in their thinking and speaking. Men usually speak overtly, saying what's on their minds in rather plain terms. On the other hand, women speak more covertly by saying things that have hidden meanings. As a hypothetical case, when a wife asks her husband if a particular dress looks good enough to wear, she might be asking him whether or not he thinks she's beautiful. The dress is of secondary importance, for her real concern is what he thinks about her.

Another difference that also complicates the communication process is the difference between the speaking-listening rate. The average person speaks at the rate of 125–150 words per minute, but we listen at the rate of 400 words per minute. That means that you can listen to what someone says faster than he can say it. Haven't you said to a person who was talking, "Hurry up and get through." You might have been saying, "I'm way ahead of you. I know where you're going and I've beat you there. Now hush so I can answer."

One consequence of this different ratio is that our minds wander, or we mentally anticipate what someone says before he says it and formulate our response. Both of these exercises can create big problems in communication.

Second, there is the communication difficulty of DEFINITIONS. Words don't always mean the same things to everyone. It has been said that words don't have meanings, just usages or connotations. Mitford M. Mathews wrote: "No word is ever used twice in just the same sense." He added, "It is a well-known fact that many words, especially those that are old in the language, have more than one clearly recognizable meaning."[13] Stuart Robertson and Frederic Cassidy wrote: "The fact is that what a word once meant is not necessarily what is now means . . . . Words, after all, are for the most part purely conventional symbols. They mean only what those who are using them agree to make them mean."[14] By upbringing and training, we often give a particular meaning to a word that is completely different from that given to it by another. Thus the very definitions of words, or the way we use them, can complicate communication.

Third, DISTORTIONS cause communication difficulties. There is always the possibility that what you say will be distorted in the sending and receiving of the message. That is, the receiver doesn't understand it in the way you intended.

John Drakeford devised a chart to illustrate the possibility of distortion in the communication of a message. He identified seven distortion points. These are: at the source of information or the brain of the sender; in the transition of the message from the brain as it is prepared for sending; during the expression of the message as it is sent verbally or non-verbally; as the message passes through the air between the sender and receiver; when the message is received by the receptor organs of eyes, ears, etc.; as the message is decoded or triggers some emotional reaction; and when it finally reaches the brain of the receiver and is accepted or not comprehended.[15] The message communicated is subject to distortion at any one of these points.

I believe that there are two major reasons for the distortion of a message. The first is our own mental conditioning. We can look for a hidden message that isn't even there, or at least wasn't intended by the sender. Furthermore, because our thought pattern is programmed to respond to a given signal in a given way, something that's said or done prompts that programmed reaction. While speaking in a part of the country I had never visited before, I was repeatedly asked, "What do you think about this area?" I developed a rather stock answer which was an accurate description of that area. Thus whenever I was asked the question, "What do you think . . . . ", it automatically triggered that programmed response. But one time the question wasn't inquiring about my opinion of the area but of the people who lived there. My mental conditioning focused on the first part of the question I'd heard so often regarding the area, and my response was that stock answer which wasn't too complimentary about the people.

The possibility of distortion is expressed in the quip: "I know you believe you understand what you think I said, but I'm not sure you realize that what you heard is what I meant."

Fourth, DISTRACTIONS can also complicate the communication process. Most of our communication doesn't take place in isolation. There are other things happening around us at the same time we are sending and receiving messages. At the same time we are subject to a variety of other stimuli—other sounds, what we see, our own physical feelings, etc. In addition, there is also the possibility that our own thought processes will distract us. Most all of us have had the experience of talking to someone whose mind or thoughts were obviously elsewhere. Perhaps you can recall some situation when you were distracted by your own thoughts and failed to receive a message.

Distractions in the home can create a real problem in communication for couples. We can be interrupted by children, or distracted by their activities. Or, we try to talk and listen with one eye and ear glued to the television. Or, we attempt to communicate while one or both mates are engaged in another activity at the same time. All of these, and more, make it almost impossible for the receiver to give his or her undivided attention to the sender.

Fifth, communication becomes difficult at times because of DECEITFULNESS. By this, I simply mean that a person doesn't always say what he means. Cecil Osborne wrote:

> "A marital problem frequently encountered involves the sending of 'coded messages.' A coded message is a communication, verbal or otherwise, which must be decoded before it can be properly understood . . . . The coded message is, in a sense, a plea for someone to meet our needs, take the trouble to understand us, to care enough to probe, pull, push, interpret, and finally get the real meaning. But this is as unrealistic as expecting someone to understand Arabic without having studied it. Communication demands an honest expression of one's feelings and needs."[16]

This deceitfulness is usually always a pitfall in marital communication. For example, a couple is invited to a party, but the husband would much rather stay home. He says to his wife, "Do you want to go, or not?" She responds, "You say." He answers, "No, it's up to you." She replies, "I'll do whatever you say." He then says, "O.K., let's stay home." So they do, but it's a very chilly evening with a frosty morning-after because the wife really wanted to go to the party.

A good rule to follow in communication is to say what you mean and mean what you say. Or, as Paul put it, "Speak the truth in love."[17]

The reality of these difficulties encountered in the communication process underscores two truths already stated. Communication is no simple exercise but instead a venture in mutual understanding which has many potential pitfalls. Furthermore, good communication is a learned skill. You and your mate need to be continually aware of these difficulties and constantly work to remove them from your exercise of sending and receiving messages so that knowing and understanding can be achieved.

Five Essential Factors

What can you as a couple do to establish and maintain good communication channels? Obviously, you must begin with a desire to know and to be known. You must also see the importance of good communication in growing and developing your relationship. Then you must be willing to work daily to perfect the skill involved in sending and receiving.

As already stated, this is easier said than done. Perhaps you saw some positive ways to do this in the previous discussion of difficulties. In seeing the areas of difficulty, maybe you also saw some ways the two of you might reduce or eliminate the danger of these pitfalls. I hope you did, but I now share what I consider to be the five essential factors for achieving and maintaining a good communication system for marriage.

Truth.—The essentialness of truth in communication is obvious. It's impossible for your mate to know and to understand you if the signals and messages you send aren't really representative of your true feelings and thoughts.

To be sure, speaking the truth doesn't mean saying everything you know or think. The admonition, "Speak the truth in love," means that we will not always say what's on our minds for in some cases this wouldn't be an act of love. However, being truthful in communication does mean that we will not knowingly or intentionally send a message that isn't representative of the situation or our feelings as we understand them. As already stated, couples often engage in the deceitful practice of saying the opposite of what they really mean or want.

Trust.—Communication demands a bond of trust. To communicate at the ultimate level of sharing your "heart of hearts," you must trust the receiver. If there's no trust there will be no real sharing of personal feelings and desires.

Why is it that many mates fail or refuse to open up to their partners? In many cases it's because they fear that what they say will not be properly received. It may be that they are afraid that the marital partners will not respect their feelings or thoughts, or will reject them. It may be that they are afraid that what they say will be held against them at a later date. All of this speaks of a lack of trust.

Such a lack of trust may be the result of a number of different factors. It could be that the person has never learned self-acceptance and thus thinks others will not accept him. Dwight Small wrote:

> "Those who say little and say it guardedly are often those with low self-valuation. They feel that to say anything will most likely expose their inadequacies and bring rejection. In varying degrees such individuals show histories of having been ridiculed, criticized, and even punished for expressing their views as children. They have been led to feel that what they have to say is unimportant, unintelligent, or uncouth."[18]

The lack of trust may also be the consequence of betrayed trust in the past.

Good communication in marriage demands that husbands and wives have complete faith in each other. Such trust doesn't demand that they always agree with each other's feelings or thoughts; however, these feelings and thoughts must be recognized as genuine. This trust also demands that they handle with utmost care the soul that's laid open in honest communication.

Time.—Good communication takes time and it often depends on the right timing. One of the casualties of our hurry-up way of living is that we don't take the time to stop and really talk to each other. How often have you said to someone, "I've got so many things to tell you, but there isn't time right now?" One study revealed that husbands and wives spent only an average of twenty-six minutes a week in serious conversation.

34

Time is an essential in good communication for three reasons. The most obvious reason is that it takes time to open up to another and share what you really think or feel. This isn't something one does on the run, or while involved in another activity. Nor are you inclined to do this when you think the receiver is too busy or preoccupied to listen.

The second reason why time is important in communication is that allowance must be made for feedback or response. Remember, communication is a two-way street. It's a channel for receiving as well as sending messages. Time must be allowed for both. In some situations, the time allowed for response must be more than the time needed for sending. The receiver needs to have time to digest and evaluate the message before responding.

Finally, time is an essential factor in communication because the right time should be chosen for the sending of some messages. There is the familiar saying, "A time to keep silence, and a time to speak."[19] The wife who greets her husband at the door in the evening with a recitation of all that went wrong for her that day isn't exercising good timing. If she makes a practice of this he will soon begin to dread coming home. It isn't a good time to deal with situations of stress when one or both of you are tired or upset.

Because time is such an important factor in communication, couples need to make arrangements to have time together. This may mean making an appointment to talk. It may mean agreeing in advance to turn off the television at a certain time, or making plans to get away from all possible distractions and interruptions on a regular basis. These "appointments for communication" should be as carefully guarded and promptly kept as an important business or club meeting.

Tact. —The necessity for tact in communication has already been indirectly stressed in emphasizing the need to choose the right time for some communication. More needs to be said about this important factor, however.

Both you and your spouse have your areas of great sensitivity. Dealing carelessly with these is much like touching a sensitive nerve—it's sure to trigger a reaction. That reaction can quickly lead to some undesired consequences. You need to learn what these sensitive areas are and stay away from them if possible, or deal with them carefully if it's not possible.

The fact is, there's more than one way to get your message

across. Suppose, for example, that your husband has an old shirt which he likes to wear around the house. You don't like the shirt and are embarrassed when someone else sees him in it. You don't want him wearing it, so how can you handle this situation (apart from throwing it away while he's at work)? You can say what you really think and feel, and tell him the shirt is a shame and disgrace, you hate it, and you think he looks like a bum in it. That's one way to let him know how you feel, but not only have you criticized something he obviously likes (since he wears it often), you've also put him down. A more tactful approach would be to say how much nicer he looks in another shirt and how attractive he is to you in that other shirt. If he's tuned in to you, he'll get the message that you don't like what he's wearing. But you will have sent the message in a manner that doesn't leave him devastated, but complimented. That's what I mean by tact.

Tact in communication is the art of saying the right thing at the right time and in the right way. That right way includes building a person up rather than tearing him down. Tact also means keeping your mouth shut about things you know are bound to trigger an undesired response on the part of your mate.

Tone.—In a sense, what you say isn't as important as how you say it. Why is it that a particular statement can be interpreted either as a put-down or an expression of affection? It's because of the tone of voice. Couples often call each other uncomplimentary names and love it because the tone of voice conveys love.

The tone of your voice in speaking can actually negate or cancel the message spoken. Mates often say things to each other that send one message while the way they say it communicates an entirely different message. One of the best ways to cause others to "disconnect you" is to speak to them in harsh and critical tones. Maybe what you're saying needs to be said, but not in the tone of voice you're using.

Communication is such a broad and comprehensive subject that any treatment of it leaves much to be said. The truths about communication I've presented in this chapter hardly scratch the surface. Hopefully, however, you've been reminded of the importance of communication in all life relationships, and especially in marriage.

Remember, communication is a skill, and as is true with any skill, it's one you need to work at constantly to improve and perfect. Study your own communication behavior as both a sender and receiver of messages. Look for better ways to send messages in order to reduce the possibility of distortion. Evaluate each message to determine if it will "build up" your partner or "tear him down." Also, in receiving messages, listen to more than just the words. Listen carefully to insure that the message you receive is the one that was sent.

If you and your mate work together in improving the skill of communication, your marital relationship will be one of continuous growth in the knowing and understanding of each other.

Endnotes:

1. Gerald I. Nierenberg and Henry H. Calero. *Meta-Talk.* New York: Pocket Books, 1975, pp. 113–114.
2. Lou Beardsley. *Put Love in Your Marriage.* Irvine, CA: Harvest House Publishers, 1978, p. 9.
3. H. Norman Wright. *Communication: Key to Your Marriage.* Glendale, CA: Regal Books, 1978, p. 52.
4. Gerald I. Nierenberg and Henry H. Calero. *op. cit.,* p. 113.
5. John W. Drakeford. *Made for Each Other.* Nashville: Broadman Press, 1973, pp. 32–34.
6. David and Vera Mace. *We Can Have Better Marriages.* Nashville: Abingdon Press, 1974, p. 104.
7. Dwight Hervey Small. *After You've Said I Do.* Old Tappan, N.J: Fleming H. Revell Company, 1968, p. 106.
8. *Ibid.,* p. 91.
9. Andre Maurois. "The Sweet Monotony of Marriage," *Ladies Home Journal.* March, 1964, p. 43.
10. David Knox. *Marriage Happiness.* Champaign, IL: Research Press, 1974, p. 53.
11. John W. Drakeford. *op. cit.,* p. 32.
12. Virginia Satir. *The Psychotherapies of Marital Disharmony.* Bernard L. Green, Editor. Glencoe, IL: Free Press of Glencoe, Inc., 1965, p. 128.
13. Mitford M. Mathews. "Meanings and Etymologies," *Essays on Language and Usage.* Edited by Leonard F. Dean and Kenneth G. Wilson. New York: Oxford University Press, 1959, p. 35.

14. Stuart Robertson and Frederic G. Cassidy. "Changing Meanings and Values of Words," *Ibid.*, p. 55.
15. John W. Drakeford. *Do You Hear Me, Honey?* New York: Harper & Row, Publishers, 1976, p. 10.
16. Cecil Osborne. *The Art of Understanding Your Mate.* Grand Rapids: Zondervan Publishing House, 1970, pp. 75–76.
17. Ephesians 4:15.
18. Dwight Hervey Small, *op. cit.*, 142.
19. Ecclesiastes 3:7.

NOTES

NOTES

3
Don't Tread On Me!

In listening to married couples talk, I've learned some things about their first fuss. I've learned that they can usually remember the reason for the first argument. Even though it may have been years ago, they still remember what it was all about. Furthermore, many couples have said that as a result of that argument they wondered at the time if they had made a mistake in getting married. The illusionary bubble had burst. The couple had suddenly realized that their marriage wasn't immune to the "down experience" of disagreement and disharmony. This realization can leave a moon-struck couple devastated.

Of course, many couples didn't have to wait until after the "I do" was said to discover that personal relationships usually have times of conflict. I say usually because once in a while I hear about a couple who claims to have a conflict-free relationship. These may be like the husband who said, "My wife and I never fuss. However, we've had some discussions the neighbors heard a block away."

Dr. Lofton Hudson has said that if two people who have lived together for twenty-five years say they have never had a cross word, you wonder what else they lie about.[1] Just what is marital conflict anyway? David and Vera Mace described it as "A disagreement, a state of opposed wills, that has been heated up by emotion—anger, resentment, hurt feelings, anxiety. The emotion is caused by frustration because you want or need something and you can't get it."[2] Conflict in marriage can range all the way from a minor and mild

41

disagreement to a major clash of wills that can quickly become verbally, and even physically, violent.

Conflict in marriage, and how to handle it, is a subject that demands attention. This is true not only because we experience it in marriage, but because it is potentially destructive. It is further true because conflict handled properly can become a means of growth in intimacy. The Maces defined conflict as a "Friend in disguise," and wrote: "Indeed, it provides the essential information the couple need for the growth of their marriage."[3] Thus conflict can definitely break or else help make a marriage. Since you're going to experience it, the choice of which it will be is yours to make.

The Crisis of Conflict

Conflict is unavoidable in marriage. Ideally, marriage is to result in a state of oneness. It has been said that in marriage two people become one and then spend the rest of their lives trying to figure out which one they've become. The fact is, however, that in spite of this oneness, you are still two separate people with your own needs and desires, your own likes and dislikes. Marriage is not a mystical union that automatically blends your distinctive personalities into one. Your differences make conflict inevitable in your relationship.

Another reason for the crisis of conflict, and one that can be avoided, is the desire of one mate to dominate the other. Mates often fail to accept each other but instead seek to dominate. Even though there is room for improvement and change in every life, a marriage license is not a permit giving you the right to make another person into someone different. This is what is often at the root of the desire to dominate. Such a move obviously results in conflict.

You should daily strive in your marriage to be accepting and accommodating, and seek to achieve a state of unity and harmony in your relationship. However, there are times when misunderstandings do arise and disagreements erupt. You cannot avoid all situations in which desires and needs clash. Thus, in spite of our best intentions and efforts, conflicts are unavoidable. H. Norman Wright wrote: "Differences and disagreements in marriage are the rule and not the exception."[4]

Conflict in marriage is, in large measure, the consequence of the current desire for marital equality. In past times, when the husband was the undisputed "head of the house" and had the one and only vote to be cast when a decision was made, there was no problem with conflict—or so it seemed. Since his will was determinative and the wife had to be submissive to it, how could there be any conflict in the marriage? On the surface there was none, but this enforced submission of the wife didn't rule out hidden feelings of resentment and hostility.

Abigail is one of my favorite women in the Bible. She was first the wife of Nabal and then later of David. She was a beauty married to a beast, and a dictatorial one at that. Little negative can be said about this gracious woman, but she did seem to resent Nabal. When Abigail told David that Nabal was, in fact, the fool his name identified him to be I think she was not only telling the truth about her husband but also ventilating some of the resentment she felt toward him.[5] Even though conflict was not permitted in her marriage, some of the emotion of it was evident.

Today we have a two-vote system in marriage. When a decision is to be made both the husband and wife usually cast a vote. Obviously, there will be times when they vote in opposition to each other, and then you have a situation of conflict.

Conflict, regardless of the cause or the occasion, and regardless of how apparently minor the issue, constitutes a crisis in the relationship. This is true because conflict is potentially destructive. Conflict can't be avoided, but if it isn't handled properly and resolved fairly it can become a force that will ultimately tear the union apart.

Years ago there was the marital joke based on a television commercial with the punch line, "We'd rather fight than switch." Not all couples who experience serious conflicts in their relationship choose to call it quits and switch mates, but a state of continual conflict destroys all chances that they will experience a mutually satisfying and fulfilling marriage. Unresolved conflict creates an atmosphere that makes it impossible for love to live, much less to grow and flourish.

James Fairchild developed a conflict chart to illustrate that unresolved conflicts do not diminish but continue to grow.[6]

Difference of opinion	"Spat"	Confrontation
Heated debate or argument	"Quarrel"	Division
Intense physical anger	"Fight"	Rejection
Hostility confirmed	"War"	Separation

43

Conflict, regardless of the cause or the occasion, and regardless of how apparently minor the issue, constitutes a crisis in the relationship.

The fact that unresolved conflicts continue to grow leads to the observation that conflict in marriage can become habitual. In discussing the types of marriages, one author identified the conflict-habituated relationship.[7] This is one in which the mates are not partners but adversaries and opponents. Every issue is approached from the standpoint of my way versus your way. Rather than the marriage being a relationship of togetherness, it is instead an armed camp filled with hostility and resentment expressed in frequent, and sometimes violent, collisions.

Therefore, any conflict is a crisis situation in your relationship. It's a crisis you can't avoid, and one that can either divide and destroy or be used as a means to greater unity and harmony in your relationship. The choice is yours to make.

The Control of Conflict

The key to handling conflict in your marriage is not to seek to eliminate it, but to learn how to control it. You cannot have a completely conflict-free relationship, but you can have one that is wholesome and growing because you have learned how to control it. This is essential if your marriage is to be mutually satisfying and fulfilling.

Atomic energy can be released in an uncontrolled chain reaction. We have atom bombs in which an explosion triggers a chain reaction that can wipe out an entire city, destroying thousands of people in a split second. But that same atomic energy can propel ships and provide electrical power to millions of homes if the chain reaction is controlled. In a similar way, conflict can result in a chain reaction that can blow a relationship apart, or it can be used to grow in understanding and love. The key is to control conflict rather than to allow it to exist in an uncontrolled state.

The control of conflict in your relationship is important because conflict involves the emotion of anger. Anger is a legitimate, God-given emotion. Even though we can develop an anger pattern or habit, it is still an automatic and natural reaction to a threat—whether that threat is real or simply imagined. In short, you cannot keep from experiencing anger, but you surely are responsible for the way you express anger.

Dennis Guernsey has developed an acrostic that helps us understand the anger process. It is A-H-E-N with the four letters representing Anger, Hurt, Expectation, and Need.[8] This anger process assumes that behind every anger there is hurt; behind the hurt there is some expectation; and behind the expectation is a need. Thus when we have a need, whether consciously or unconsciously, there is the expectation that it will be met. In marriage, we usually look to the mate as the one to meet that need. When the expectation that the need will be met is not fulfilled, we become hurt. Hurt then leads to anger. This process confirms the conclusion that "Anger is a secondary emotion; there is always another emotion behind it that caused it."[9]

In conflict situations in marriage one or both parties often become angry. Thus the situation of a clash of wills, or disagreement, is complicated by the emotion of anger. This further mandates the control of conflict, for unrestrained anger can be most destructive.

There are some essential elements in the control of conflict. These will make it possible for you to keep the inevitable conflicts in your relationship within livable limits as well as to make them stepping stones in the growth process.

First, the control of conflict involves having some ground rules for conflict situations. Since it is true that you're going to experience some conflicts in your marriage, why not decide in advance how you're going to handle them? Just as boxers need to have an arena or ring in which to fight, so marital disputes ought to be limited by certain rules and agreements. These rules may simply be an agreement to freely talk and listen to each other when you disagree, rather than withdraw and clam up. Or it can be a more complex plan to defuse the bomb of conflict before it explodes.

When couples have mutually agreed what to do when they disagree, they are in a better position to deal with disputes when they arise. Furthermore, because the agreement about how to handle conflict was mutually made, one partner can kindly remind the other of the rule if it's not being followed.

Second, the control of conflict also involves good communication. This is a complex and basic part of a good relationship, as expressed in the previous chapter. Communication is a key in controlling conflict, for if you bury anger in the basement of your life by suppressing or repressing it, your partner is left in the dark about the severity of your feelings. To make matters worse, this anger easily turns into resentment which makes its ugly presence known in any one of a number of undesirable ways.

Finally, the control of conflict demands self-control. The only way to keep conflict from becoming a damaging and destructive chain reaction is to keep a tight hold on the leash of self-control. This isn't always easy to do, particularly when your emotions become heated. When we are attacked or threatened, the natural inclination is to counter-attack and strike back. When we are hurt we usually want to hurt in return. Obviously, this is a response which doesn't work to the resolving of the situation but instead accelerates it into a full-scale war.

When we're under emotional stress, we often say things and sometimes act in ways that hurt the one we love. These actions are usually not indicative of our deepest and truest feelings, but are expressive of the emotions and frustrations we feel at the time. We are immediately sorry, but the words have been spoken, or the deed has been done. One of the most ridiculous things some of us do then is say, "I take it back." I'd like to see you reach out into space—or in another person's heart and mind—and take back a word spoken. Further, once something is done it cannot be undone. Regrettably, these hastily and thoughtlessly spoken words and deeds are not quickly forgotten.

I often counsel couples to remember two important things about words spoken in the heat of an argument. First, we are often guilty of saying things we really don't mean. You see, we're hurt, and as I said before, when you're hurt you usually want to hurt in return. Since we know that physical violence is taboo, especially toward the one we love, we're often guilty of resorting to verbal violence. We often say what we really don't mean. Therefore, couples need to learn not to take too seriously the things said in the heat of an argument.

Second, I caution couples to remember that once they've said something it remains said. Even though you can, and should, immediately say, "I'm sorry," and give assurances that what you said is not what you really feel or believe, the fact is, it was said. Even though a bad experience should be put behind us and forgiven, especially when there has been an apology, it's not quickly forgotten. It often takes time for the hurt to heal. Thus you need to keep a guard on your tongue. Do whatever it takes—count to ten, take a deep breath, call a momentary halt to the confrontation, or whatever—but at all costs keep your tongue under control!

The Conduct for Conflict

When people find themselves in a conflict situation they often react in one of two general ways. These are either withdrawing or winning. In withdrawal a person retreats from the fight. Some people withdraw physically by leaving the room or the house. Others withdraw psychologically by not speaking, ignoring the situation, or just insulating themselves so that what is happening has no penetrating power.

Withdrawal is often a self-defense tactic. The person is hurt and in an attempt to avoid still further hurt to himself, and not wanting to hurt in return, he simply withdraws and, in effect, tries to pull a protective shield around himself. On the surface this may seem to be a good way to act in conflict. After all, it takes two to fight, and by withdrawing you're making a fight impossible. The problem with this, however, is that the issue which caused the conflict or the hurt is left hanging rather than being resolved. Furthermore, as already stated, the initial hurt that prompted the withdrawal is only stored up in the basement of your feelings where it can fester.

Some couples develop the habit of responding to conflicts by withdrawing. Since one withdraws from the fight, there can be no fight. Nothing is left for the other partner to do but withdraw also. So like two weary fighters, they each retreat to their own corners to glare at one another in stony silence. They sit there, waiting for emotions to subside sufficiently to go on with a bare semblance of a relationship until the next experience of conflict, all the while storing up more and more resentment toward each other.

The second general reaction to conflict is to go on an all-out offensive to win the battle at the expense of losing the war. We live in a highly competitive society in which a premium is placed on winning, and a loser feels stigmatized. Winning is considered to be necessary in order to maintain self-esteem. As H. Norman Wright put it: "To defer to another, to give in, or to lose a debate or argument is a strong threat to the person's feelings about himself, and thus he fights so that this will not happen."[10]

The problem with this approach to conflict is that in marital conflicts there should be no winner versus loser. Either both win or both lose. You can go all out to win the argument, thus defeating

48

your mate, but if you do you both lose in the end. Or else, you can handle the conflict in a way that allows both of you to win. Your goal in conflict should be "To communicate honest feelings of anger, frustration, and confusion."[11] Doing this in the right way allows your mate to understand what is happening inside you. Then, if the partner responds in a proper way to this communication, something can be done to resolve these problems and both of you are then winners.

Having identified these two general ways some couples react to conflict, I hasten to add that there are situations when these two reactions of withdrawing and winning are combined into one sequential action. In this a person "hits and runs." He unloads his hurt or hostility in a manner that says, "I'm right and you're wrong," and then he retreats without allowing for any feedback or response.

In the marital relationship both withdrawing or going all out to win at the expense of another are strictly taboo. To leave your mate in the dark about your true feelings, and to want to win at the expense of the one you love, are not acts of love. After all, lovers are not to see each other as enemies or opponents.

What, then, is the proper conduct for the crisis of conflict? I offer the following practical words of advice. If these are followed they will enable a loving couple to defuse the bomb of marital conflict and actually make it work for them by becoming a means for growth in their understanding of each other. Conflict then becomes a means of achieving the desired goal of intimacy in marriage.

First, make sure that you understand the situation. So many disputes are the result of some misunderstanding. It's easy to misunderstand what was said, or misinterpret some act. Longfellow reminds us that, "Things are not what they seem."[12] You can easily see a meaning that's not even there. To be sure, an imagined threat is as real to the person as a legitimate one. But to react to a threat that's imagined and not real is to perceive a conflict situation where one didn't even exist.

Another reason why it's necessary to understand the situation is that aggressive action by your mate may well be the expression of frustration that doesn't even relate to you, or something you did or didn't do. Richard L. Strauss wrote: "We must remember that angry attacks against us are sometimes provoked by exasperating incidents totally unrelated to us. Often when husbands and wives are irritable, their mates just happen to be the most convenient target for their angry outbursts."[13]

To be sure, taking frustrations and hostility out on an innocent bystander isn't fair, but if you as the target of such aggressive behavior understand what's happening you shouldn't feel personally threatened. Thus there is no need for you to retaliate, but instead you are in a position to help your partner get over whatever is bothering him.

Take the time to try to understand. See if there are some extenuating circumstances. Are there some hidden issues which, if understood, will lead you to react differently? Is he unusually tired or troubled about something? Is this the wrong time of the month for her? Dr. Theodore Reik used the phrase, "the third ear."[14] He means the ability to "hear" feelings and meanings that are hidden. As indicated in the chapter on communication, we often send coded messages which say one thing but mean something entirely different.

Second, deal with just one issue at the time. I've heard of counselors who advise their clients to avoid all confrontations until a predetermined time and then deal with all the issues accumulated over a period of days. Quite obviously, there are times when couples must wait to deal with some issues. After all, a fuss in front of strangers, friends, or even the children, is a bit embarrassing. Furthermore, some issues may be so minor that by putting them on hold for awhile you forget all about them. Thus further conflict may well be avoided by delay.

All this being true, however, I don't see how couples can effectively deal with one conflict if they are trying to address a dozen different ones at the same time. You would almost need a traffic cop to keep the situation from becoming a hopeless jam.

Don't gunny sack your conflicts, storing them up inside you until they build up so much pressure that you go off like a sky rocket. Don't dump an accumulated load of gripes and grievances on your unsuspecting mate. Instead, deal with one issue at a time. Once that issue is resolved, do with it what is normally done with dead things —bury it and let it be, not to be resurrected and hashed over at some future date.

Third, attack the issue and not the individual. One of the greatest faults in our interpersonal conflicts is that we lash out at each other, leaving the issue involved virtually forgotten. It isn't a case of two

50

people seeking to resolve some point of disagreement, but two combatants hammering away verbally at each other in disagreeable ways.

H. Norman Wright related the story about a sheepherder in Wyoming who observed the behavior of wild animals during the winter:

> "Packs of wolves, for example, would sweep into the valley and attack the band of wild horses. The horses would form a circle with their heads at the center of the circle and kick out at the wolves, driving them away. Then the sheepherder saw the wolves attack a band of wild jackasses. The animals also formed a circle, but they formed it with their heads out toward the wolves. When they began to kick, they ended up kicking one another."[15]

It is so easy in an argument to become excessively critical of your mate and make hasty and inaccurate judgments. We read all sorts of ulterior and sinister meanings and motives into what they've said or done. Attacking them with these charges inspires a counterattack, and the war is really on.

One helpful way to deal with the issue and not attack the individual is to make "I" statements rather than "you" statements. "I" messages are attempts to express our feelings without blaming, name calling or brow beating another person.

Wright wrote: " 'I messages' are messages that identify where the speaker is and thus are more oriented to the speaker than to the listener . . . . an 'I message' is distinguished from a 'you message' in that the speaker claims the problem as his own . . . . It is a statement of fact rather than an evaluation and, therefore, less likely to hurt the relationship."[16]

Fourth, speak the truth in love.[17] As previously stated, in marriage your partner is not to be seen as an enemy, and you shouldn't treat him as such. Maybe your mate is wrong in what was said or done, and it's necessary to point this out, but don't do it with all the sternness of a judge imposing a sentence, and certainly not with the tone that says, "Aha! I'm right, and you're wrong!"

Fifth, quickly seek and grant forgiveness. Marriage can't be based on perfection, but it must involve the behavior of forgiveness. Conflicts are inevitable, and they are frequently sharp and divisive. The issue must be resolved and forgiveness must be sought and freely granted. Richard L. Strauss wrote: "It is impossible to overestimate the importance of forgiveness. When we grant forgiveness, resentment and bitterness disappear and our harsh and intolerant attitudes are replaced with genuine love and concern for our mates."[18]

Forgiveness must also involve forgetfulness. Psychologists state that a person never really forgets anything. All our past experiences are filed away in the brain, consciously or unconsciously. But once something is forgiven, it is to be put in the past and left there. Continually to bring up incidents you say you've forgiven isn't fair and makes your forgiveness a joke.

If you are in the wrong, quickly admit it and ask for forgiveness. If you are the person wronged, grant forgiveness, even if it isn't requested. Only through the process of forgiveness can the process of healing take place.

In summary, here are some workable ways to resolve points of conflict in your marriage: keep anger under control; be honest in sharing your feelings; guard carefully what you say; avoid "blame" statements; listen to what your partner is saying and be sure you're hearing correctly; focus on one problem at a time; be alert to other forms of communication; be ready to forgive. These are easy to list but are difficult to do. If you learn how to do them, however, you'll be able to defuse the bomb of conflict and make it work for you.

A little girl heard the story of Cinderella for the first time. She went home and told the story to her mother. When the child got almost to the end of the story, she stopped and asked, "Do you know what happened then?" The mother answered, "They lived happily ever after." "No, they didn't," the child responded. "They got married!"

The little girl seemed to think that getting married and living happily ever after are not the same. For millions of couples this is tragically true. One of the reasons why is that they have never learned how to deal with conflict. Instead of using the inevitable conflicts in their relationship as stepping stones in building a better marriage and achieving the goal of intimacy and understanding, they are constantly guilty of treading on each other. What you do when conflict rears its head will determine, in a large measure, the kind of relationship you will have.

Endnotes:

1. Henry E. White. "Handling Family Conflict," *Home Life.* Nashville: August 1977, p. 16.
2. David & Vera Mace. *We Can Have Better Marriages.* Nashville: Abingdon Press, 1974, p. 89.
3. *Ibid.,* p. 87.
4. H. Norman Wright. *The Pillars of Marriage.* Glendale, CA: Regal Books, 1979, p. 135.
5. 1 Samuel 25:25.
6. James G. T. Fairchild. *When You Don't Agree.* Scottsdale PA: Herald Press, 1977, p. 19.
7. H. Norman Wright. *op. cit.,* p. 15.
8. Dennis Guernsey. *If I'm So Free How Come I Feel Boxed In?* Waco, TX: Word Books, 1978, pp. 105–106.
9. David Mace. "When Christian Couples Get Angry," *Home Life.* Nashville: November 1981, p. 38.
10. Wright. *op. cit.,* p. 147.
11. Richard B. Wilke. *Tell Me Again, I'm Listening.* Nashville: Abingdon Press, 1973, p. 95.
12. Longfellow, Henry Wadsworth. "A Psalm of Life," *The World's Best Loved Poems,* compiled by James Gilchrist Lawson. New York: Harper & Row, Publishers, 1955, p. 194.
13. Richard L. Strauss. *Marriage Is for Love.* Wheaton, IL: Tyndale House Publishers, 1973, p. 92.
14. Theodore Reik. *Listening with the Third Ear.* New York: Farrar, Straus and Co., 1949.
15. H. Norman Wright. *Communication: Key to Your Marriage.* Glendale, CA: Regal Books, 1978, p. 145.
16. H. Norman Wright. *The Pillars of Marriage,* pp. 155–156.
17. Ephesians 4:25.
18. Richard L. Strauss. *op. cit.,* p. 96.

NOTES

NOTES

NOTES

4
The Bedroom Blessing

If you could listen to what some couples say in the counseling room, you would wonder why I've called this chapter on sex in marriage, The Bedroom Blessing. The way some couples talk about their sexual relationship indicates that it's anything but a blessing.

It's tragic that what God intended to be a beautiful and pleasurable experience in the relationship of a man and a woman can, in fact, become an experience in which there is so much confusion and conflict. This is what the sexual relationship is for many couples, however. Sexual incompatibility is ranked third in a list of the ten most common problems in marriage.[1]

In many modern marriages sex is not a blessing. Quite to the contrary! For many it is a bad scene with undercurrents of frustration, resentment and hostility. In other marriages sex is a routine ritual devoid of real satisfaction and enjoyment. One psychologist stated that "The most common complaint (about sex) is boredom. Couples get used to a habitual love-making routine and quite naturally lose interest."[2] Another counselor wrote that "A common complaint of the married is the lack of novelty or creativity in sexual relations."[3] One young wife expressed this boredom to me when she said, "Sex is not a big deal with us. We can take it or leave it."

The fact is that the Lord God created us as sexual beings.[4] Sex isn't something you do for you are a sexual being and your sexuality is expressed in all you do and say. As a sexual being, you have the possibility and permission to relate intimately and sexually in marriage.

Before going further in this chapter it's necessary to establish a definition and define a viewpoint. First, what is meant by the word sex? Obviously, the word has many different meanings today. Sex is used to identify gender, the genital organs, sexual intercourse, or a basic life force. Since this chapter deals with the physical relationship of husband and wife, I shall use the word to refer to both the possibility and the performance of a sexual relationship.

Second, it is possible to deal with the subject of sex from two different viewpoints—the secular and the sacred. The first sees sex as simply a biological function and frequently divorces it from any moral considerations. From the secular viewpoint, sex is simply a matter of "doing what comes naturally." The second viewpoint— the sacred—sees sex as a God-given need to be expressed and fulfilled within definable limitations. These limitations serve to heighten rather than diminish the sexual relationship.

I choose to deal with the subject from the sacred viewpoint. I do so, not just because of my professional orientation, but also in the awareness that since God made us sexual beings with the ability to express our sexuality in the physical relationship of marriage, He knows best how to make the most of His gift.

God Said, "It's Good"

The place to begin any discussion of sex in marriage is at the beginning. As stated above, we are sexual beings with the capacity for a sexual relationship because that's the way the Lord God made us. Furthermore, God liked what He did and called our maleness and femaleness good.[5]

It may sound strange to say that sex was God's idea. After all, there's so much exploitation of sex by the entertainment and advertising media, so many expressions of human sexuality that result in scarred and ruined lives, and so much negative approach to the sexual side of life by otherwise well-meaning people. But sex was His idea, and the idea is good. To seek to reject our sexuality, or deny sex the place it has in life, is to attempt to renounce God's creative purpose.

It isn't my purpose in this chapter to present a study of the scriptural teachings about sex, but I would summarize in several statements what the Bible teaches about marital sex. The following statements are fully supported by both Old and New Testament teachings:

> (1) The husband and wife both have sexual needs and desires which are to be fully satisfied in marriage.
> (2) The "Act of Marriage"[6] (sexual intercourse) is approved by God as an expression of love, an exercise in oneness, an experience of pleasure, and for the purpose of procreation.
> (3) In marriage, the person's body belongs to the mate and should be a source of delight and pleasure for the marital partner.
> (4) Both partners in marriage are forbidden to refrain from meeting their mate's sexual needs unless it is by mutual consent.

Since sex was God's idea, and He approves of our sexuality and the proper expressions of it, what are the purposes of sex in marriage? These were touched on in the above statements, but they need to be more clearly defined and understood.

First, sex is for PROCLAMATION. There is no more beautiful or exciting way for a man and a woman to declare their love for each other than in the "syntax of sex." "Making love" is a common expression for intercourse. Actually, sexual togetherness is not to be an exercise in "making love" but giving love. Making love sounds mechanical. Tragically, that's what sex is for many couples, for it's a duty performed with routine regularity without any tenderness or affection. I believe that sex without love in marriage is as much a prostitution of God's intention as is sex with a prostitute.

I pointed out in the first chapter that one of our most basic life needs is to love and to be loved. The ultimate human fulfillment of this need is experienced in marriage. In the marital relationship you and your mate are to experience love as both the giver and the recipient. And the most precious way this can be done is in sexual intercourse. Professor Jon Nilson wrote:

> "If the spouses love one another and they prove it by trying daily to make each other feel wanted, content, secure, and treasured, their lovemaking will be pleasurable—but very much more besides. They will often experience their sexual intimacy at a special time when they give themselves totally to

Both husband and wife have sexual needs and desires. These needs are not experienced in the same way or with the same regularity, but they both have them.

each other and when they receive the awesome gift of each other's whole person. Boredom will rarely find a foothold in them for their delight in each other's openness and availability will leave no room for it. What happens between them will reveal and express the depth of the love they show each other in so many other, more ordinary ways throughout their days together. In their lovemaking, they will experience more completely and intensely what they already experience in the ebb and flow of their everyday life. In this special time, each is there for the other totally—body, mind, and heart—for no other reason but to express the fulness of their love. So when they come together, the true story of their shared love is being told."[7]

Thus God gave us sex for the purpose of proclaiming love. Sex without love makes it simply a biological exercise or an animalistic activity. This purpose of proclaiming love should undergird and be expressed in all the other purposes of sex in marriage.

Second, sex is for PLEASURE. The unhappiness and frustration experienced by so many couples in their sexual relationship is the exact opposite of what God intends. One of the oldest Biblical commands about marriage reads: "When a man is newly married, he shall not go out with the army or be charged with any business; he shall be free at home one year, to be happy with his wife whom he has taken."[8] The phrase, "be happy," speaks of the pleasure to be experienced in a sexual relationship.

The ancient Hebrews were far more open than most of us in their approach to the man-woman relationship. They wrote in descriptive details about the pleasurable aspects of a sexual relationship. As an example, consider these words about sexual love (from Proverbs): "May your fountain be blessed, and you rejoice in the wife of your youth. A loving doe, a graceful deer—may her breasts satisfy you always, may you ever be captivated by her love."[9] One whole book in the Old Testament—the Song of Solomon—was written for the purpose of extolling the beauty and pleasures of sexual love.

Furthermore, understand that the pleasure to be experienced in sexual relations is not intended to be one-sided. It is not to be a matter of one partner getting a thrill at the expense of the other. Lou Beardsley, in her book, *Put Love in Your Marriage*, wrote: "Somehow, through the years, various old wives' tales got started that sex was only for men's enjoyment and the women were simply 'the victims' of their husbands' animalistic behavior."[10] Regrettably, this is the way it is in many cases and both the husband and the wife are the losers. Women are to experience sexual pleasure also. In fact, one part of the female sexual anatomy has no function whatever other than being the focus of sexual pleasure.

Third, sex is for POSSESSION. In the first chapter I emphasized that marital love involves a feeling of belonging. Certainly one aspect of your becoming one is that each of you belongs to the other. This belonging has a physical dimension in that you not only belong to each other in the sense that you've committed yourselves to each other, but in that your very bodies become your mate's property.[11] "Sexual love is so vital to Christian marriage that God removes the rights of the individual to control his or her own body."[12] This purpose of possession is expressed in sexual intercourse as each of you gives your body to the other. You are thereby objectifying the fact that you do belong to each other.

Finally, sex is for PROPAGATION. I mention this last, not to minimize the importance but because it is the most recognizable purpose for sex. It is by means of sexual intercourse that man reproduces himself. This is also a part of God's plan, for He told the first couple to be fruitful and multiply.[13]

This purpose of sex is also mentioned last to emphasize that there are other legitimate purposes. You see, there are some people who accept no purpose for sex other than procreation. J. H. Kellogg, a physician and inventor of corn flakes, wrote a book in which he stated that man demonstrates the depths of his depravity when he engages in intercourse for any reason other than procreation.[14]

Sex is for procreation, but this purpose is to be used with discrimination. Just because God gave you the ability to bear children doesn't mean you should have as many as you can. Choose your own method of birth control, but have a method. It is wrong to have a child you don't want, for it's every person's right to be wanted. Furthermore, you should not have more children than you can adequately provide for.

Is Sex That Important?

Now there's a question that would spark up the conversation at some get-together. In fact, Dear Abby received "literally bushel baskets of mail" on that subject. A wife who was tired of sex wrote Abby and asked that the readers of her column be polled on their feelings about sex. Even though there were thousands of responses in favor of sex, the dissidents wrote the most replies. One woman's reply stated that, "Sex is much ado about nothing."[15] She signed her letter, "Alone and Happy." With an attitude like that, I know why she was alone!

Well, is sex that important? I say, "Yes!" To be sure, sex isn't the most important part of marriage, but it can become that if you have problems adjusting sexually.

There are several reasons why I say that sex in marriage is important. First, it is because sex is a basic reason for marriage. Don't misunderstand me at this point. I'm not saying that the reason people should marry is in order to experience sexual satisfaction. The primary motive for marriage should be a love in which two people want to give to each other rather than a desire to get from each other. However, sex is a part of that giving, and if it wasn't for sex there would be no need for marriage at all.

We have marriage because we are sexual beings with the ability to relate intimately with members of the opposite sex in a sexual relationship. Ruel Howe said, "Sex needs marriage and marriage needs sex."[16] Thomas Bland put it: "Man's capacity for sexual communion with the opposite sex makes marriage possible; man's readiness for sexual sin makes marriage necessary."[17] Therefore, sex is important because if it wasn't for sex we wouldn't have marriage in the first place.

Second, sex is important in marriage because it determines the kind of marriage you have. Good sexual relations don't guarantee a good marriage, but poor sexual adjustment can destroy a marriage and will certainly keep it from being a fulfilling and satisfying relationship. I've said that to couples in scores of counseling situations, and it's true! If things aren't right between a couple in their bedroom, they will not be right in any other room of the house.

It's true that "man does not live by bed alone"—not even in marriage. But if things aren't right in the area of life represented by the marital bed, that becomes a loose thread that can eventually unravel a marriage. Professor Nilson wrote: "What happens in the bedroom is often a mirror of what is going on between husband and wife in the rest of their life together."[18] One wife candidly acknowledged, "I can always tell when we aren't sexually active enough, because we start sniping at each other. It's a fact. Both our temperaments are better when we're sexually active."[19]

For emphasis, I repeat this fact: A good sexual adjustment alone doesn't make a good marriage, but it's necessary if you're going to have a good marriage. Now what and how much constitutes a good sexual relationship for you and your mate is up to the two of you to decide together. There is no hard and fast rule to follow. Each couple is free to determine what is good for them. The important thing is to mutually determine just what you want and don't want, and how much is enough. But it's important for you to do that—and do it mutually! One contented mate, plus one frustrated mate, equals one problem marriage.

Third, sex in marriage is important because the husband and wife both have sexual needs. Furthermore, they have every right to express their needs and expect them to be met in their marital relationship. The sexual needs of husbands and wives are not necessarily experienced in the same intensity and usually are not experienced with the same regularity. As one marriage counselor said, "The wife's need is more-or-less cyclic, while the husband's remains fairly constant—forty-eight days a month." Despite their differences, however, both husband and wife do have sexual needs and this makes sex in marriage important.

The husband has the need to love his wife sexually. In a sense, the very fact that she is there and is attractive to him, creates that need. The man's sexual desire is related to vision. When he looks at his wife, especially when she's fixed herself up, and finds her attractive, he automatically has sex-oriented thoughts and may desire to love her sexually. Men are turned on by feminine nudity, or peek-a-boo glimpses of semi-nudity. Wise is the wife who understands this and keeps her husband interested in her by keeping herself physically attractive for him, as well as allowing him the visual excitement of her body.

A part of the husband's need for sex is physical in that he needs to have periodic sexual release. Males experience an accumulating physiological pressure which demands release. The Lord God so designed a man that this release is a must for him if he has no physical, emotional or psychological problems. This sexual release is vital to a man's outlook on life. As a wife, you need to remember that a satisfied man is a contented man, but a frustrated one will blow up over almost any incident, no matter how insignificant. As one husband put it, "When our sexual relations are good, nothing she

64

does annoys me. But when they aren't almost everything she does bugs me."

Some of the husband's need to love his wife is psychological. A man's ego—how he sees himself—is closely related to his sex drive. If a man is frustrated in his desire to love his wife physically, either by his own failure or by her rejection of him, he will experience a rapid decline in self-confidence in other areas of life as well. But, if he is allowed to be the lover he needs to be, and the wife is sexually responsive to him, he will feel as if he could climb Mt. Everest.

Also involved in the husband's sexual need is his need to be loved by his wife. Even though the Lord God equipped the man to be the aggressor and initiator in the man-woman relationship, a man needs to know that his wife is excited by him and desires him sexually. She can convey this to him by her responses to his advances, as well as by taking the initiative herself at times. There's nothing in the marriage vow that says a wife has to wait to be wanted. She can become the initiator by letting her man know that she wants him.

Now, let's look at the other side of the picture. The wife has the need to be loved sexually also. To be sure, her need is not as physically oriented as the man's. Her need is closely related to her emotions. In short, a woman needs to be romanced. Husband, romance to your wife doesn't mean just getting into bed together. It's all you do before you get into bed and that causes her to want to get into bed with you. George and Margaret Hardisty described this romance:

> "Romance is when a man says to a woman, 'You're a doll, you're beautiful, you're the only one in the world for me.' It's a touch of the hair as you go by...uhh...gently. It's when you reach over and squeeze her hand in church. It's helping her on with her coat and opening doors for her. It's when you leave a note on the bathroom mirror or call her two or three times during the week from work. 'Just because I was thinking of you.' Romance is a gift from you that she wouldn't buy for herself, like a music box or a special teacup. It's 'unspecial day' gifts like a rose, or a box of pretty soap. Romance is telling her you love her, a MINIMUM of once a day. It's taking her out to dinner to a really nice place even if you have to save up your nickels to do it."[20]

As the responser, the woman's desire is related to assurances that she is loved. She responds to being held and caressed in loving ways. Women are stimulated primarily by the sense of touch. Dear wife, if you will allow your husband to hold you close, as well as fondle and caress you lovingly, you will discover that your desire for him will rise to equal his for you. However, if you deny this closeness, or fail to communicate to him your need for it, you will be left out and he will fail to be the lover both of you want.

A part of the wife's sexual need is related to her self-esteem. James Dobson has pointed out that low self-esteem is the number one problem with most wives.[21] He further stated that one reason why low self-esteem is such a big problem with wives has to do with physical attractiveness.[22] This feeling of low self-esteem can be alleviated to a great degree by husbands. If you, as a husband will be expressive of your love for your wife—meaning verbal affirmations as well as physical attention—she will have little reason for a poor self-image. A husband can make his wife feel she is the most special person in the world—at least, to him. When a woman thinks positively about herself she will be a better lover.

There is also a physical side to the wife's sexual need. Even though her sex desires may not be as constant or regular as the man's, it may well be as intense. Recent research indicates that the intensity of pleasure and sexual excitement at the moment of climax is about the same for both sexes.[23] Furthermore, studies in human sexuality reveal that women "are capable of greater sexual response both in terms of frequency of intercourse and degree of orgasm."[24] Added to this is the fact that the woman's sex drive increases as she grows older. Since the woman's response is learned, her capacity to enjoy sex increases.

Even though there is no physiological pressure demanding sexual release in a woman, as is true with men, sexual climax for a woman does result in the relaxing of her nervous system. Even though there are exceptions, fretful women are usually lacking in a satisfying sexual relationship.

Thus sex is important in marriage because both the husband and the wife have sexual needs and desires. These needs are not experienced in the same way or with the same regularity, but they both have them.

One additional word needs to be said about the importance of sex in marriage because of our sexual needs. That word is about the possible consequences of failing to meet each other's need. A poor sexual adjustment in marriage doesn't give husbands and wives permission to seek sexual satisfaction outside the marriage, but it surely does open the door to that possibility. As one satisfied husband put it, "When you have a Cadillac in the garage, how can you be tempted to steal a Volkswagen off the street?"[25] But when one mate repeatedly denies the other sexually without cause, that mate is virtually inviting the other to find someone else.

Ways to Make It Great

Repeated emphasis has been given to the fact that marriage is what you make it. This is true not only of your relationship in general, but also of the various areas and expressions of your relationship. Your sexual relationship will also be what you make it. How the two of you accept yourselves as sexual beings with sexual needs, and how you respond to each other at this level of life, determines just how great your sex life will be. In other words, just because sex is for marriage, and the two of you have said "I do," doesn't automatically mean that sex will be great for you.

Men and women enter marriage with the necessary equipment for a sexual relationship. But using it in a manner that becomes mutually satisfying and fulfilling is a learned process. It has been said that the most important sex organ is the brain. This means that sex is more mental than physical. It also means that for your relationship to be all that God intends requires correct knowledge and understanding.

Sometimes the place to begin this learning process is by unlearning. Many people enter marriage with the wrong information and a lot of misconceptions about sex. What has been learned in locker room "bull sessions" or at slumber parties is usually far from the truth.

For sex in marriage to be great it must be positive, peaceful and pleasant. By POSITIVE I mean that it is to be an expression of love and a desire to give. Even though each of you has your own sexual needs and certainly wants them satisfied, your primary concern should be the needs of your mate. If both of you approach your sexual relationship in this positive manner, neither of you will be the loser.

Then, by PEACEFUL, I mean that sex must be relaxed and unrushed. We live in a hurry-up world in which we often rush around at top speed. But a sexual experience is not to be a hurry-up affair.

It is true that a man can become quickly aroused and almost as quickly experience release. But, husband, this isn't true of your wife. Sexual arousal is a gradual process for her, and after the peak of sexual excitement she wants to be held and further assured of your love. This requires time. The most recent studies reveal that it only takes the average man 2.8 minutes of sexual stimulation to reach a climax, but it takes the average woman 13 minutes of stimulation to have orgasm.

In addition, the peaceful requirement for great sex also means that it's to be without stress and interruptions. The latter requires making some arrangements, but the former is more difficult to deal with. Neither partner should feel the stress of having to perform in an undesired manner, or of feeling that it's necessary to prove sexual prowess or ability. In fact, the very thought that this must be done can actually short-circuit the delicate sexual function.

Finally, by PLEASANT, I mean that sex must be mutually enjoyable and satisfying. Does this mean that both mates are to experience a sexual climax, and that simultaneously? Absolutely not! The simultaneous climax as the height of sexual compatibility and adjustment is a myth. Furthermore, a time of loving togetherness can be fulfilling even if neither partner achieves a climax. That is, it can be if both understand that this isn't always necessary.

Having identified these three characteristics of great sex— positive, peaceful and pleasant—I hasten to point out that these are the results of right attitudes and activities in effecting a good sexual adjustment. What are some of these attitudes and activities?

First, learn as much as you can about each other. Understanding your own sexual needs and desires is not the same as understanding your mate's needs and desires. Furthermore, discover the erotically sensitive areas of your mate's body so you will know the places to touch that give the most pleasure. You can learn about your mate in two ways. One is by reading books containing factual information about male and female sexuality. A second way to learn about your mate is by talking to each other openly and honestly about your sexual feelings and desires. Don't be like thousands of couples who experience years of marital misery because of lack of understanding and misunderstanding regarding sexual needs and desires. Even though it takes effort to overcome initial shyness, loving your mate should demand this of you.

Second, make your own rules. I have touched on this already, but an additional word is needed. No two couples are the same. Various studies of sexual activity report the average number of times couples "make love" each week. These studies often report statistically on various techniques used in sexual relations. Don't fall into the trap of thinking you're not normal if you don't fit the average. Forget about quantity, or how many times a week you should make love, and major on quality. If you do this, the quality will take care of the quantity.

Couples often ask, "What's normal in marital sex?" The answer is, whatever the two of you want to do. The Bible teaches that the marital bed is undefiled.[26] That means that whatever a couple wants to do in the expression of their love, and in their desire to give and receive pleasure, is all right. There are only two exceptions to that rule. One, you must mutually agree on what you do, and two, neither of you is to be hurt in any way.

Third, allow your mate freedom with your body. After all, the sexual relationship involves a physical activity. It is important that each of you be excited by your mate's body. Remember, in marriage your body belongs to your mate. That fact means nothing, however, if you enforce a "hands off" policy when it comes to allowing your mate freedom with your body.

Allowing body freedom can be a problem for men as well as women. However, it's usually more of a problem with wives. Don Meredith wrote:

> "It is generally much easier for a man to develop freedom with his body and with his mate's body. Women are not as free as men sexually. They compare themselves with the youthful, unblemished bodies of models on TV, which results in great insecurity. . . . Some women believe that the lower parts of their bodies are extremely unattractive and even unsanitary. . . . Yet men, when polled on what part of their wife's body was most attractive, overwhelmingly said the genital area."[27]

Dear wife, you need to remember two important things about your body. The first is that your husband is sexually stimulated by what he sees. That's why sex shows cater to men and are primarily attended by them. Since a man is stimulated by what he sees, and there are plenty of places for him to go to see, it's up to you to provide the visual stimulation he craves. The second fact you need to remember is that your sexual desire is stimulated by touch. If you, as a wife, deny body freedom to your husband, you are not only denying him the joy of being excited by you, but you are also denying yourself the enjoyment of your own sexual feelings.

It is written that Adam and Eve were "naked and not ashamed."[28] They were not encumbered by centuries of erroneous negative programming that taught that there's something evil about the body. The ideal in your sexual relationship is to recapture the wonderment and excitement of our first parents—naked but not ashamed.

Fourth, learn how to say, "No." I believe a good rule to live by in marriage is not to say no unless it's necessary. Maybe a wife doesn't feel the need for sex when her husband makes an advance. However, if she loves him, she should want to meet his need even if she isn't in need of sexual release herself. Husband, if you love her, you won't take advantage of such a willingness on her part by making advances when it's obvious it isn't a good time for her.

There are times when a negative response is in order. It isn't a good time; she really doesn't feel well; there isn't enough time; he is worried about something. In such times, "No" can be spoken in a way that leaves the mate feeling rejected and devastated. Or, it can be said in a way that says, "Not right now, please, but later." Martha Shedd wrote:

> "It used to really bother me when Charlie would come home from work and start playing around while I was getting dinner. My first reaction was, 'For crying out loud, Charlie, not now!' So he would go away rejected and then I would feel guilty. This went on and on, and we were getting nowhere. . . . Then one night I decided to try something different. I turned and put my arms around him and said, 'Charlie, you're getting me so excited, I can hardly wait. See you in bed.' Well, he went away and read the paper and instead of feeling negative toward each other, we were both looking forward."[29]

Finally, never use sex as a reward for "good behavior," or a means of punishment. Sex is an expression of love, not a right to be earned or a reward to be given. Even though we usually don't feel loving when we're disappointed, and we do want to show appreciation when we are pleased, to use sex as a means of punishment or as a reward definitely cheapens it.

This isn't all you can do to make your sex life positive, peaceful and pleasant, but it's a start. If you and your mate will at least start with these ways, you will discover more yourselves—and the discovery will be wonderfully exciting. Remember, the key is, it's what you make it. It's up to you to keep your sex life exciting and make the bedroom symbolic of a great blessing in your marriage.

Endnotes:

1. Claire Safran. "Troubles That Pull Couples Apart," *Redbook Magazine*. January, 1979, p. 83.
2. Daniel Araoz. Quoted by Eric Faucher. "1 in 2 Marriages Has Serious Sex Problems," *National Examiner*. July 6, 1982, p. 35.
3. David M. Thomas. "Blending Marital and Religious Experience," *Marriage and Family Living*. Vol. 64, No. 5, May 1982, p. 19.
4. Genesis 1:27.
5. Genesis 1:31.
6. Tim and Beverly LaHaye. *The Act of Marriage*. Grand Rapids: Zondervan Publishing House, 1976.
7. Jon Nilson. "The Liturgy of Sex," *Marriage and Family Living*. Vol. 64, No. 6, June 1982, p. 13.
8. Deuteronomy 24:5 (RSV).
9. Proverbs 5:18–19 (NIV).
10. Lou Beardsley. *Put Love in Your Marriage*. Irvine, CA: Harvest House Publishers, 1978, p. 22.
11. 1 Corinthians 7:3–4.
12. Don Meredith. *Becoming One*. Nashville: Thomas Nelson Publishers, 1979, p. 173.
13. Genesis 1:28.
14. Harry Hollis, Jr. *Thank God for Sex*. Nashville: Broadman Press, 1975, p. 29.
15. "Dear Abby" *Jackson Daily News*. Jackson, Mississippi, Monday, August 25, 1980, Section B, p. 2.
16. Harry Hollis, Jr. *op. cit.*, p. 61.
17. Thomas Bland. "Toward a Theology of Marriage," *Review and Expositor*, LXI. Spring, 1964, p. 8.
18. Jon Nilson. *op. cit.*, p. 12.
19. Charlie & Martha Shedd. *Celebration in the Bedroom*. Waco, TX: Word Books, 1979, p. 18.
20. George & Margaret Hardisty. *Honest Questions–Honest Answers*. Irvine, CA: Harvest House Publishers, 1977, pp. 17–18.
21. James Dobson. *What Wives Wish Their Husbands Knew*

About Women. Wheaton, IL: Tyndale House Publishers, 1975, p. 22.
22. *Ibid.,* p. 26.
23. *Ibid.,* p. 117.
24. Dennis Guernsey. *Thoroughly Married.* Waco, TX: Word Books, 1975, p. 86.
25. Tim & Beverly LaHaye. *op. cit.,* p. 19.
26. Hebrews 13:4.
27. Don Meredith. *op. cit.,* p. 187.
28. Genesis 2:25.
29. Charlie & Martha Shedd. *op. cit.,* pp. 78–79.

NOTES

NOTES

5
To Buy Or Not To Buy?

A businessman in my city has a one word explanation for the cause of marital problems and divorce. That one word is money. Even though money is not the only cause of disharmony in marriage and divorce, it is a cause. The problem of having too much month left over at the end of the money can put a real strain on the husband-wife relationship.

Just how serious is the money issue in marriage? Money ranked second in a Redbook survey of the most frequent problems for couples in their twenties.[1] The study showed that "Counselors report an increase in the number of conflicts over money, and they blame the rocky state of our national economy."[2] Similar studies show the same. George H. Gallup reported that money was the chief source of quarreling between husbands and wives. Joyce Brothers stated that "American couples argue far more about money than any other issue." Richard L. Strauss wrote that it has been estimated "That at least sixty percent of all married couples have had some degree of conflict over money."[3] That estimate is probably low.

Financial problems in marriage have been around a long time. In one sense, the strain related to financial difficulties can be traced back to the first marriage in history. Adam and Eve never had to stretch a pay check, meet monthly installments, or deal with past due notices, but the desire to acquire got them into a lot of trouble. That desire has been intensified in a material way by the abundance of consumer products readily available in stores and by mail-order, plus the attractive and alluring advertising techniques of Madison Avenue. These, coupled with easy credit and buy-now, pay-later plans, have made it very easy for couples to find themselves owing more than they make. The obvious consequence is strain and tension that detrimentally affects the couple at virtually every level of their relationship.

A fundamental question in this milieu of money matters is (with apologies to Shakespeare's "Hamlet") "to buy or not to buy?" This issue demands that the two of you, as a couple, sit down together and take a long hard look at how much you have to spend, what should come first in the disbursement of the funds available, and then decide what you really need as opposed to what is a non-essential luxury. This exercise takes in a lot, and that's what this chapter is about.

Financial Follies

I've heard it said about some people that they have no sense when it comes to money. It isn't my desire to judge others, and certainly not to judge you. However, I have to admit that the way some folks are about money does indicate that they do lack good sense.

One big financial folly of our time is the prevailing wrong idea about the importance of money. Some comic said, "Money isn't the most important thing in the world, but it sure beats what's second." Our society, with its materialistic orientation and concepts, keeps money before us as the number one priority in life. People are measured in terms of their earning ability and we often think that the person who has more is worth more. These false concepts have led millions of people to put making money as the goal of their lives. In an on-the-street interview a reporter asked a man, "What is the purpose of life?" The man quickly replied, "To make money!"

With this wrong attitude about money, people have come to two equally wrong conclusions. The first is that if they only had more money all their problems would be solved. Maybe you have jokingly said, "I have no problems that a million dollars wouldn't solve." There are folks who have millions, however, who would be quick to say that money isn't a magic potion that cures all ills.

The second erroneous conclusion that results from our wrong attitude about money is that it's the source of happiness. People have said, "I'd be happy if I just had all the money I want." But they wouldn't be. Having a lot of money just enables you to be miserable in a better part of town.

A second major financial folly is one that's more likely to be a danger to you in your marriage. It's the folly of allowing money to control your marriage. It has been said that money is a good servant but a terrible master. Money will become your master if you put it first and don't control it.

Even though there are a number of ways by which money can become a controlling factor in your marriage, there are two definite ways you need to guard against. If you fail to do so in either of these ways the result will be that you will be a slave and money will be your master. These two ways I warn you about are greed and excessive debt. They are listed in that order because greed can easily lead to excessive debt.

Let's look first at greed. It is often called the "Judas problem."[4] Greed exists because of the "more syndrome." That is, what you have isn't enough —you want to have more.

Greed can be traced back to the first married couple. Eve looked at the forbidden tree and desired its fruit. Even though she and her husband had the whole garden and all its luscious, fruit-laden trees to enjoy, that wasn't enough for Eve. She wanted more, and with greedy grasping, she took more.[5]

The same principle operates today. More and more things are readily available to us. These are often attractive and alluring. Furthermore, there's never a shortage of voices saying, "Go ahead, take it! You deserve the best! Don't deny yourself!" Before you know it this desire to acquire will become a consuming power in your life that results in a constant state of discontent with what you have. Money will have become your master.

The second way that money takes control of your marriage is by excessive debt. Money takes control in the form of an intolerable, oppressive debt when your grasp for things exceeds your ability to pay for them.

The subject of debt is difficult to deal with. After all, our national government has operated for years on the principle of deficit spending—spending more money than it takes in. You are in serious trouble when your outgo exceeds your income. To say the least, a life lived under the oppressive hand of creditors isn't conducive to a wholesome, enjoyable marital relationship.

Marital Money Management

Managing your money is the key to seeing to it that your money doesn't control you and your marriage. Robert Hastings wrote: "The ultimate aim of money management is not to save, but to build our spending around healthy goals."[6] Whether money is your servant or master is determined by whether or not you manage it. That's easier said than done, however. It may be fairly simple for a single person to handle his or her finances. But when there are two of you the process can become complicated. Additional management problems develop when the two of you become three, and more.

Having stated that money management is the key in determining whether you'll control your money or be controlled by it, I quickly add that in order to manage your finances properly some major decisions must be made. I believe there are three issues in the management of your finances. If you and your mate can get together—and stay together—on these three issues, you'll be well on your way to building a financially stable marriage.

First, recognize that God comes first with your money. That recognition is based on the fact that God is the owner of everything and we simply have temporary use of what we have. Putting God first puts money in the proper perspective. The wise man of old observed that the best policy with money is to honor the Lord God with a portion of it. He wrote: "Honor the Lord with your substance and with the first fruits of all your produce; then your barns will be filled with plenty, and your vats will be bursting with wine."[7] I would add that even though the Bible commands giving, your primary motive for putting God first in the expenditure of your funds should be gratitude for His goodness to you. Furthermore, even though you shouldn't take a legalistic approach to giving in that you expect a "full barn" or a full pocket in return, the fact is that you'll be blessed. I believe that if you give God the tithe (a tenth), as well as an offering expressive of your love for Him, what you have left will go further.

Some couples say they can't afford to tithe. My wife and I learned a long time ago—as newlyweds living on military pay— that we couldn't afford not to tithe. Elsie Stapleton made a study of two hundred families who gave away at least one tenth of their incomes. She was impressed by the discovery that she didn't find a

Managing your money is the key to seeing to it that your money doesn't control you and your marriage.

single one of those families operating "in the red." They were well-adjusted spiritually and financially. She observed that "They knew the value of money, and they spent their earnings on what was most important to them. The ten percent tithe was the most vital of their outlays."[8] The fact is that what you have left after the tithe will go further than the entire amount when you keep the tithe.

Second, plan a household budget and stick to it. A budget is a projection of expenses based on anticipated or known income. It's a plan for meeting your financial obligations and providing for the things you need and want.

A household budget can accomplish several important purposes in the management of your finances. One, it enables you to keep control of your spending. Couples frequently cash their pay checks and then a few days later sit down and try to figure out where the money went. Usually they discover that by not having any means of control they spent some of the precious funds foolishly. By means of a budget you can plan in advance where the money should go. By following that plan you not only know where it went, but you are able to see to it that money is not foolishly spent.

Two, a budget helps you choose a suitable standard of living. Your standard of living must not be chosen on the basis of the standard of your friends. They may have a larger or smaller income than you. When a couple takes stock of what they have coming in, thus knowing what their spending limit is, they can then plan for the disbursement of funds in line with their resources. This process results in determining a standard of living in keeping with your income. It will keep you from waking up one morning to discover that you're living far beyond your means.

Three, having a budget makes it possible for you to provide for the future, or to purchase something special both of you want. By means of a budget a couple can put some money aside for a rainy day, a special project, or a vacation trip.

As previously indicated, your budget must be tailor-made to fit the needs of your marriage and family unit. Furthermore, your budget should go through constant revision and updating. Therefore, no set budget can be worked out for you by another, but I do offer a procedure to follow in planning your household budget.

In general terms, your budget should have two divisions. The first can be called Fixed Expenses. In this section of the budget you will list items and amounts over which you have no control. These include such things as mortgage payments, rent, insurance premiums, etc. As a Christian, the tithe should also be listed in this section. These items should be listed and budgeted first.

The second division of your budget can be labeled Flexible Expenditures. These are items over which you do exercise control. That is, you can determine how much or how little you'll spend for these items. These flexible expenditures will include such items as groceries, utilities, clothing, savings, travel, etc.

Two additional words need to be said about your budget. Be sure that you budget money to cover unforeseen expenses. If you own anything mechanical, or are buying a house, there is always the possibility that it will break down, or need to be repaired. A sudden repair bill can wreck the best budget. Also, since some insurance premiums are paid quarterly or semi-annually, each month take one-twelfth of your budgeted amount for these premiums and put them in a savings account. This has two definite advantages for you. Obviously, that money will be working for you earning interest, plus the fact that when the premium is due you don't have to come up with a large amount of money.

The last decision to be made in the matter of money management involves the question of who should control the pursestrings—the husband or the wife? This is a point of sharp conflict in many marriages. The question is often complicated by the situation of both spouses having an income.

There are two errors which need to be pointed out initially. The first is having separate bank accounts rather than a joint account. The second is dividing the household expenses with the husband paying some out of his salary while the wife is responsible for the others out of her income. Neither of these practices is healthy in building a harmonious relationship. After all, marriage is an exercise in oneness, and I believe that should include finances as well as every other area of marital life. You're asking for trouble when you take a "yours versus mine" approach to money. Even though each partner should have some pocket money, or an allowance for incidentals, the family treasury should be "ours." Men, this is true even if the wife doesn't work outside the home. Think of the predicament you would be in if you had to pay someone to do all she does in keeping the home fires burning!

The decision of control is largely taken care of if the two of you together have planned a household budget. When both partners have worked together in developing a budget it really makes little difference who writes the checks. If there is no budget, however, the decision of control becomes a major one.

Two words of advice are in order at this point. One, it is best if only one person has the responsibility of managing the budget, including writing the checks. Keeping up with your bank balance and staying up-to-date with your obligations becomes a difficult task if more than one person is writing the checks. Certainly your mate should have the right to sign checks on your joint account, but it is best to have just one person as the primary check writer. Two, husband, if your wife doesn't work outside the home, and you are the one who manages the household budget, it's a good policy to give her a set amount of money each week for her use. She shouldn't be held accountable to you for what she does with this money.

What about special or major purchases, even those provided for in your budget? I firmly believe that the decision "to buy or not to buy" should be jointly made. The wife who isn't consulted by her husband before he purchases an item of major expense (unless it's a gift for her) is made to feel she's not important and what she thinks doesn't matter. The husband, whose income may be the family's only or primary means of support, who is left out of a major purchase decision may well come to feel that he's nothing but a paycheck to his wife.

It is easy to see why the issue of who will manage the household finances is easily a source of hurt feelings, resentment and hostility. Here, as elsewhere in your marriage, the bottom line must be mutuality. Both marital partners are to have input and the final decision about management and all it involves must be mutually made. The decision is not the same for every couple, but it must be a couple's decision.

Priceless Principles

In the preceding sections of this chapter I sought to warn you about some financial follies that can have a detrimental effect on you and on your marriage. Also I pointed out three essential activities in good marital money management.

Having said all that, however, there is still that question, "to buy or not to buy?" Determining the right answer to the question in each situation is not always easy to do. Certainly there is no one answer which fits all situations. Sometimes the answer will be yes,

82

sometimes no, and sometimes wait. However, I believe there are principles that can be applied in each situation to help you determine whether you should buy or not. These principles are priceless, not only because of what they may eventually save you in dollars and cents, but also because of the peace of mind that comes from knowing you did the right thing.

First, be cautious in buying. There are times when you really shouldn't make the purchase in question. By being cautious you can be spared the folly of foolish spending that might put you in a financial bind. There are other situations when you'll decide to make the purchase and by being cautious you can make certain you're getting the best deal possible.

Caution in purchasing involves a number of very practical exercises. I simply spell out a few of these with a minimum of commentary or elaboration. One, be wary of "something for nothing" schemes. A person who offers to share his secret for making a million dollars with you for a donation of ten dollars is probably making his million dollars with the ten dollar donations of gullible people. "Get rich quick" schemes and "something for nothing" gimmicks are just that—schemes and gimmicks. Be wary of them!

Two, take time before deciding to buy. You can buy in haste and repent in leisure. It's really frustrating to grab an item off the shelf hastily, fork over the required price, and then on the way home pass by another store where the same item is for sale for less. Furthermore, if you take time to sleep on some purchase involving a major expense you may wake up to realize that the item is not something you really want or need, at least right then.

Three, shop around. Manufacturers set suggested retail values on their products, but the individual merchant can set his own price. The same article may be on sale in another store for much less. A word of warning is in order, however. Don't sacrifice quality for price. A cheaper product can be very attractive, especially when funds are limited, but if it won't last as long it can be more expensive in the long run. A good example of this is furniture. A chair is a chair, or so it may seem; therefore, why pay more for one when cheaper styles are available? In the long run you will probably save money by purchasing a better quality item because it will last longer. This principle of quality versus price also applies to clothing, as well as to a number of other items you need.

Four, don't be pressured into buying. There is a difference between buying something and being sold something. The first activity indicates individual choice while the second implies pressure. If you have to be sold it may well be that the product in question is one you don't want or need.

Five, remember that some products and services will cost you more than you initially think. The price tag on the article or fee for the service may not include all you have to pay, or will want. Maybe you heard about the wife who purchased a new pair of shoes at a sale for a greatly reduced price. Then she felt she had to go out and buy a whole new outfit to go with her new shoes. That's an exaggeration, but it illustrates a truth. The sticker price on a new automobile doesn't list such additional costs as tax, title fee, interest on notes or the amount it will cost to operate the vehicle. You may decide to move into another apartment because the rent is cheaper, only to discover that the utility expenses are higher, or you need new curtains, etc. Therefore, before making your decision of whether to buy or not to buy, look for the additional expenses that aren't readily seen.

Sixth, before you make the purchase or close the deal, ask yourself, "Do I really need this? Is this something I really want?" Such questioning as this can be a money-saving exercise whether the item in question costs one dollar or one thousand dollars. Asking such questions can also save you unnecessary expense when you're living on a very limited income.

The second principle that will help in the issue of buying or not buying is to be content with what you have. I don't mean that you should put up with just anything, especially if you're able to provide something better, but I do mean that you shouldn't live in a state of constant discontent with what you have.

Admittedly, this recommended state of contentment isn't easy to achieve or to maintain. After all, look at all the shiny new products available in the marketplace. Shopping malls are crammed full of goodies just waiting to be gobbled up by compulsive shoppers. Added to this is that constant verbal and visual pressure in the form of commercials and advertisements. One business author recently estimated that the average American encounters about 2,000 sales messages a day.[9] These messages not only promote products, they also sow the seeds of discontent. They tell us that the newest is the best; thus, what you have isn't good enough. The message is that last year's car is inferior to the latest model; last season's clothes are not in keeping with today's styles; the "old" appliance is obsolete because it doesn't have the latest technological gadgetry.

You are wise indeed if you learn the secret of contentment. Don't be content to put up with just anything, but at the same time don't be discontent with what you have just because it isn't the latest or most expensive model available.

Furthermore, be content with your answer to the question, "to buy or not to buy?" Once you've made up your mind and acted on your decision, accept it and go on. People often make themselves miserable by wondering if they did the right thing after they've done it. I am guilty of this myself at times. Having made a major purchase, I've had the experience of wondering, "Should I have bought this?" My enjoyment of the product purchased has been nullified for a time by these second thoughts. Once you've considered everything involved in a possible expenditure of your funds, and reached the best decision you can make at the time, be content with it. Don't keep looking back over your shoulder, doubting your decision.

Money isn't to be the most important issue in your marriage. Your relationship to each other as husband and wife should have priority over everything else except your relationship to God through Jesus Christ.

Even though money shouldn't be the most important thing in your marriage, it can easily become just that. John C. Howell wrote: "Too many couples spend most of their waking hours earning money to purchase more possessions but do not take time to build a better marriage."[10] In the end both lose in spite of all they've gained. To paraphrase a familiar passage of Scripture,[11] "What shall it profit a couple if they gain all they want and lose their own marriage?" In every community there are houses of magnificent design with luxurious appointments which are nothing but mausoleums for dead marriages.

Will that be true for you? It's possible, for money, including the pursuit of it and problems with it, can wreck a marriage. Here again the key is how the two of you deal with the matter. In this area, as well as in every area of your life together, your marriage will be what you make it.

Endnotes:

1. Claire Safran. "Troubles That Pull Couples Apart," *Redbook*. January, 1979, p. 138.
2. *Ibid.*, p. 139.
3. Richard L. Strauss. *Marriage Is for Love.* Wheaton, IL: Tyndale House Publishers, 1973, p. 101.
4. David L. Hocking. *Love & Marriage.* Eugene, OR: Harvest House Publishers, 1981, p. 126.
5. Genesis 3:1–6.
6. Robert J. Hastings. *How to Help Yourself.* Nashville: Broadman Press, 1981, p. 97.
7. Proverbs 3:9–10 (RSV).
8. Elsie Stapleton. *Spending for Happiness.* New York: Prentice Hall, 1949.
9. *Bits and Pieces.* Marvin G. Gregory, Editor. Fairfield, NJ: Economics Press, Vol. 13, No. 9, September, 1980, p. 24.
10. John C. Howell. "Under Attack: The Christian Home," *Home Life.* Nashville: November, 1982, p. 6.
11. Mark 8:36.

NOTES

NOTES

NOTES

NOTES

NOTES

NOTES